SURVIVAL

A Manual on Manipulating

SURVIVAL

A Manual on Manipulating

WILLIAM M. JONES

PRENTICE-HALL, INC.
Englewood Cliffs, New Jersey

Prentice-Hall International, Inc., *London*
Prentice-Hall of Australia, Pty. Ltd., *Sydney*
Prentice-Hall of Canada, Ltd., *Toronto*
Prentice-Hall of India Private Ltd., *New Delhi*
Prentice-Hall of Japan, Inc., *Tokyo*
Prentice-Hall of Southeast Asia Pte. Ltd., *Singapore*
Whitehall Books, Ltd., *Wellington, New Zealand*

© 1979 by
PRENTICE-HALL, INC.
Englewood Cliffs, N.J.

Library of Congress Cataloging in Publication Data

Jones, William M
   Survival : a manual on manipulating.

   Includes index.
   1. Psychology, Industrial.   2.   Persuasion (Psychology) 3. Influence (Psychology) 4.   Communication in
management.   I.   Title.
HF5548.8.J559 1979   650'.13   79-16011
ISBN0-13-879114-7

Printed in the United States of America

PREFACE

Early in the 1960s I was in Washington on business when a friend asked me to talk to a group of executives at the State Department about communications theory from an academic point of view. The group's response to my talk was so positive that I was soon making frequent trips to Washington to discuss communication problems in government management. Wherever I went, from the Department of Transportation to the U.S. Information Agency, I found everyone bemoaning the breakdown of communication in executive management. "How can we expect to get adequate appropriations from Congress," one agency director said to me, "when the people in one section of our agency don't understand the work the others are doing?"

As I came and went between university campuses and Washington agencies, I set myself the task of studying communication patterns among executives to find out how they could be improved. At NASA headquarters in Washington, and later around the country at such installations as Cape Kennedy and Marshall Space Center, I watched the shrewd operators negotiating for larger and larger budgets for their projects, sometimes sacrificing other parts of the program to get themselves a larger chunk. At the National Institutes of Health I saw some of the same crassness in operation. Gradually, in my three-week executive training sessions I brought together small groups of executives from different government agencies who were anxious to improve their oral communication techniques. I constructed what I call my "airport cocktail lounge" atmosphere. The casual, transitory setting made for open, uncompetitive discussion.

I soon began to find an answer to that agency director's question about communication failure. Very few of the top executives in my training sessions had ever realistically admitted what they were after and what they were willing to do to achieve their goals. They had been trained in some discipline but had no guided experience in the kind of manipulative interaction required of them as participants in big government management. When I branched out and began similar training sessions in big business, I saw the same absence of any realistic understanding of interpersonal relationships at the professional level.

Back on my own university campus, I again found that the failure to regularize manipulative practices accounted for much of the communication failure, with specialists bumping into one another in their efforts to succeed. Seeing the need for a comprehensive guide to realistic manipulative techniques, I began making notes on my conversations with executives around the country.

This book is the result of that investigation. It is filled with case histories that have been thoroughly mixed and distorted to hide the identities of those whose successes and failures in the manipulative game served as my starting point for a guide to control through manipulation. Although I had originally planned the book to be a defensive guide for protection against manipulators, I discovered that such a one-sided approach was impossible. Anyone who plans to work in industry, government, or any organization composed of three or more people must accept the impossibility of playing a passive game.

I express my gratitude to the hundreds of serious-minded

professionals who contributed to the writing of this book, especially to Eric Valentine, whose editorial encouragement helped me to shape it into something far more ambitious than I had originally envisioned. In keeping with standard practice, I have tended to use masculine pronouns throughout; but the world of business is no longer unisexual, and the consequences of that change can be seen in a book to which male and female executives have contributed equally.

WILLIAM M. JONES

CONTENTS

INTRODUCTION
Uncle Alex and Corporate Gratitude

W HEN I was growing up in Alabama, Uncle Alex was the man I admired most. First of all, he lived in Birmingham, the center of things. He had been to college and was the family success. He was a business executive! By the time I was in high school, he had been transferred to St. Louis—up north—with an impressive salary. When he came home to visit his mother, we'd gather around the table and hear his stories from the world of big business. He was honest, loving, gentle with everyone. Everybody liked Uncle Alex.

While I was away at college, Uncle Alex came home for good. He and his wife settled down in his mother's house, in the room that he had left for success. An administrative reorganization had saved his company money and had cost Uncle Alex his job. At 54 he was glad to take a job as night clerk in a hotel owned by a friend from high school days. He said to me, his eyes so close to tears that I looked away from him, ''I gave them my life, and they weren't even grateful.''

His mistake? He had been trained to believe that organizations have memories and are capable of emotions such as gratitude. If Uncle Alex had worked with his eyes open, he would not have expected from a fluid, impersonal organization something it was not constructed to give. Individual people have emotional capabilities; corporate structures do not. They are a constantly fluctuating mass of sections, boards, and committees that encourage the impersonal to hide the painful.

This book is for Uncle Alex—and all those who gave more than they got. It is not for romantic idealists who would lash out to transform the system instantly. Such people will benefit from this book only after they learn to look unflinchingly at present possibilities. This book is for realists who want to survive within the present system while retaining a modicum of personal dignity and integrity.

Such realists will find that I have made an honest effort to report on standard practices in big businesses and government agencies. Nothing I have observed has shocked me; after Uncle Alex came home, I was shockproof.

What I offer is a rational, unemotional analysis of the way manipulation works in business and government, a guide to help business executives survive, emotionally and psychically, in their public lives. To those who argue that such manipulation dehumanizes, I reply that dehumanization occurred a long time ago. Now manipulative skill can help us regain our humanity. Only when we know the rules of the game can we distinguish fair play from foul. In a heated basketball game you don't meditate on the "humanity" of the player you pass the ball to. He may be a husband or father or criminal, but at the moment he is the best place to throw the ball. So it is with manipulation; you are not dehumanizing but expressing your humanity through energetic, controlled play.

Those involved in corporate life have two choices. They can manipulate power with as much intelligent awareness as possible and derive some satisfaction from controlling their own days, or they can be manipulated by others until they become frustrated objects, their humanity destroyed by their own directionless hatred.

No one with any hold on reality can deny that manipulation is a way of life. When two people come to a narrow doorway, one of them is going to go through it first. One of the two will make that decision. At the doorway the one who assesses the available choices and decides is exercising power. Such conscious management of another person—such manipulation—builds self-confidence and reinforces awareness of the need for manipulation. Whenever choice is required, someone will decide. Better you than someone else!

Manipulation
Theory

1

THE PHILOSOPHY OF MANIPULATION
Working with Reality

MANY of America's managers are depressed because the techniques they have learned are not working. "I try hard," they tell me, "to be honest and sincere. I never shirk my responsibilities; I take work home nearly every night. Yet I see other people moving ahead while I'm stuck in the same rut." After several years these managers are embittered and cynical, deeply disappointed because they have not achieved the success they were led to believe honesty and hard work would get them.

From talking to such managers—and the successful executives they work for—I have learned that the hard-work-and-love philosophy does not apply in today's impersonal business world. Those executives who are still trying to run their careers on outmoded principles are being given less and less to manage.

The term "management" has come to mean shrewd, realistic manipulation. In a complex business environment everyone is both manager and managed, manipulator and manipulatee. To survive in such an environment, we must free ourselves of idealistic half-truths and work intelligently with clear-sighted realism. When we hear people giving lip service to an outmoded ethical system, we should nod in wise agreement but realize that they are probably trying to manipulate us for some purpose of their own.

Whenever money, power, and influence are at stake, someone is going to control them. In earlier days control was concentrated among aristocrats and a few super-rich capitalists. Those days have given way to a system that offers masses of managers a chance for some degree of control. The people who study the power structure and their relationship to it have a better chance to succeed than those who actually believe the regulations promulgated in dittoed departmental memos and annual board reports.

Wherever you are in the power structure, it is better to be smart than stupid. A quiet young man moving upward in a government agency once told me, "The clever old-timers at the top find me useful. My pure idealism is a nice cover for their dirty work." With such wise innocence this young man manipulated his superior manipulators.

Grabbing Hold

That alert young idealist had already begun to see the nature of manipulation. He realized that it is as much a part of human behavior as sex and eating. Mothers control their children with no-no's and slaps. Adolescents manipulate each other with coy glances and gentle touches. Business executives control each other in more complex ways, but their success depends, as always, on making people do what they want them to do. That's manipulation.

The two general types of manipulation are *personal manipulation* and *organizational manipulation.* Both individuals and organizations can be manipulated by appeals to their weaknesses. Learning how to spot those weaknesses is the key to successful manipulation and is the subject of the next two chapters.

Manipulation of both sorts can be viewed in terms of the manipulator's relationship to the manipulatee: upward, lateral, or downward. *Upward manipulation* is practiced on more powerful superiors. Successful executives expect a certain amount of judicious fawning from their subordinates. They endured the debasement process on the way up; now it is somebody else's turn to cringe. Their attitude is similar to that of fraternity brothers who advocate continued hazing of pledges. "Because we had to" is the rallying cry of the successful conservative.

Since such manipulation is expected, beginners need to know where "up" is. A misunderstanding of the geography of the upper regions can lead to wasted effort or a damaged career. Dan, for example, spent a great deal of effort flattering his section chief, two echelons above him. Dan's immediate superior resented Dan's bypassing him. Too late Dan discovered that the section chief, who had accepted Dan's attention, would do nothing for him professionally without the recommendation of his immediate superior, who had the pleasure of labeling Dan uncooperative and delaying his promotion.

Upward manipulation is usually confined to the next-higher level. Occasionally, when a competitor is working that level, or when you can prove your immediate superior is incompetent and replace him, it is possible to move two steps higher. But this kind of manipulation works best with frequent, close association. Too high too fast may lead to a downfall.

Lateral manipulation is practiced on equals. Since a large part of manipulation is careful observation, lateral manipulation—which gives you more opportunity to study your subjects—is a good place to begin practicing manipulative skills. It is safer to make your first mistakes on your equals rather than on your superiors.

Lateral manipulation, sometimes jokingly referred to as "screwing your buddies," is as necessary as war games at an army training camp. When the real opportunity comes along, the good manipulator has had plenty of practice under sheltered conditions. You and your equals can play harmlessly together like puppies, romping and snarling as you practice attack and defense. Unfortunately, on occasion some villain becomes serious and changes the mood. At that point you sound the battle alert and start playing for keeps.

Downward manipulation—the control of subordinates—is less dangerous than upward manipulation. But don't assume that because people make less money than you they can do you no harm. The built-up hatred of a nameless subordinate you have unknowingly slighted can cause more unpleasantness than the momentary wrath of a tolerant superior.

This kind of manipulation can consume enormous amounts of time. Be sure that you don't spend hours chatting and drinking coffee with people less powerful than you just to inflate your own ego. Your role as superior can shift very quickly from manipulator to manipulatee. If you know what you are doing, a little ego boost is all right; but once you've satisfied your ego, you'd better get back to work on more rewarding kinds of manipulation.

One of the main values of downward manipulation is that it provides you with a broad information base. You can open up a communication system that channels valuable gossip your way. You should certainly use downward manipulation to arrange for hearing the suspicions and half-truths swirling in the lower depths. You can also use your base to distribute information. Coffee, lunch, or cocktails with those who look up to you can be a fine opportunity for dropping tidbits about yourself or others that you want to seep upward to the right ears. Details, even when somewhat garbled, are more impressive when filtered through an unbiased, impersonal source.

A section head told me about his "wave theory" of communication. He pointed out that small waves, washing constantly against a granite cliff, can eventually cause it to crumble. He sends constant waves of information outward from around him, carefully controlling them so that they follow each other to the high executive shore. Gradually, he says, those seemingly impregnable cliffs will be so leveled that he will be able to walk ashore at any point he chooses. This executive's wave theory has yet to be proved incontrovertibly, but he has done very well so far. Wherever you are in your organization, you can send out vibrations to make your presence known in the right circles at the right time.

Sending out waves is only part of the total manipulation process. The major activities in manipulation are collecting information and developing relationships. You should view yourself and your associates as if you were moving constantly up and down in a bank of parallel elevators. Managerial success depends on a continuous reassessment of these fluctuating relationships. Some executives draw elevator charts while talking on the phone so that they can have a clear picture of where they are at that particular moment in relation to the person on the other end of the line.

Directional manipulation of the kind we have been discussing is essential in both personal and organizational manipulation plans. Wherever it is used, it must be accompanied by a total understanding of the manipulative process so that you are in control at all times.

Hanging On

The manipulator's ultimate goal is power control. Such control begins with self-discipline. It requires constant alertness to opportunities and awareness of appropriate techniques to use on specific occasions. Many managers develop a stock response to daily routines. Gradually, their professional lives become uncreative and dull. They let the deadening effects of the environment control them until they respond automatically and sometimes disastrously.

One executive picked up his phone to find that someone was on the line. Assuming it was his secretary, as it usually was, he said, "Get off the phone, damn it! I want it." The person on the phone was his boss. The consequences of this lack of self-control were not immediately obvious, but the executive came to be labeled an unstable hothead—largely on the basis of this trivial incident.

Good manipulators never respond automatically to any situation. With creative, controlled energy, they see the choices available to them and others. Such clarity of vision gives them self-confidence along with self-control. That confidence comes from pacing themselves so that they don't push faster than they can easily move.

You don't drive safely at night beyond the reach of your headlights. You don't drive yourself during the day beyond the reach of your self-control. If someone presses you for an immediate answer, resist the temptation to make a hasty decision. "I'll have to check my records" or "I'll let you know tomorrow" can protect you from being the object of someone's manipulation—someone whose purpose may include pushing you too far.

The coolest head survives the chopping block longest. Losing control may sometimes be an effective manipulative device, but shrewd manipulators lose their temper, shout, cry, or blaspheme only when a dispassionate appraisal of the situation suggests that is what is needed.

Most people are manipulated because they are scared, passive, or insecure. Any of these emotions deadens their sensitivity to choices and weakens their possibilities for control. When people are debilitated by insecurity, the situation often resolves itself through apathy and inactivity. At such times managers say, "Well, there's nothing we could have done about it." Or, more frequently, "If we had only known!"

Self-control can help you to know. And it is self-generating. Once you become aware of your ability to manipulate, your self-confidence activates your self-control. Hang on to your self-control, and you will control those who control the power. That's as functionally useful as controlling the power directly.

The only danger is that your confidence may grow more rapidly than your knowledge and skill. When such an imbalance occurs, you are thrown out of control and your hopes are shattered. Every "Nothing ventured, nothing gained" should be accompanied by a "Look before you leap." Realistic manipulation requires a constant balance between fear and foolhardiness. Overconfidence is as harmful as lack of confidence. But with realistic observation you can rapidly develop an awareness of your capabilities and the manipulative possibilities open to you. The confident manipulator knows when to give a little push and when to take one quietly.

Giving and Taking

At times you have to work aggressively to manipulate others. At least as often you must use your knowledge of manipulation for self-defense. *Aggressive manipulation* is most effective when you are moving in a new direction or striving for a new position. The rest of the time you should be prepared to use *defensive manipulation* for protection against those who want to use you. If you remain inattentive for long, an aggressive manipulator gains control. At such times you will have to construct a quick defense or develop an active counterattack.

Harry was transferred to a congenial department with a stable, closed power structure. Only by destroying the present pattern could he advance. He began by gently complaining that Fred was mistreating him. The older employee was left with the choice of doing what he was accused of—cutting the man down—or doing nothing and being accused of the same thing. The more he tried to be pleasant to Harry, the more Harry spread the word of Fred's vicious hypocrisy. Soon Harry was replacing Fred at conferences and assignments because of the sympathy his aggressive manipulation had generated.

In this situation Fred's integrity was a handicap. He should have recognized Harry's aggressive behavior and discredited him with defensive manipulation. An early, public confrontation might have saved Fred a great deal of suffering. Manipulators who cultivate false attitudes are often intimidated by a direct challenge. They prefer to work with whispers. Open defense will shatter their fragile fabrications. What Fred lacked was the sensitive observation that is often the best defense. The one who sees the patterns first usually calls the shots.

But how, you ask, could Fred have known what Harry was doing to him? By realizing, without bitterness or disillusionment, that action is not necessarily indicative of intention. Whenever one of your co-workers stands to gain from a change of position, you have to be on guard. Fred's first error was the usual one in managerial situations: complacency. He had become blind to the possibility of change in his position. Plodding conscientiously along, he assumed that he would always continue at the same pace in the same direction.

An aggressive manipulator can tilt your landscape so that you are suddenly climbing desperately uphill or, worse, slipping backward. Fred should have put his Early Warning System into operation as soon as a new personality entered his vicinity. He should have used upward manipulation to improve his communication ties with superiors. Or he should have strengthened his downward relationships, so that a concerned secretary with whom he occasionally chatted would have let him know that Harry was knifing him. Instead, Fred let his insensitivity to reality blind him to the necessity of developing manipulative techniques. He thus became pitifully vulnerable to Harry's aggressive manipulation.

If Fred had known immediately about Harry's slander, he could have brought it to the attention of sympathetic superiors, who could have dealt with the situation. Sometimes, even more active cross-slandering is necessary to neutralize aggressive manipulators. When they see they have met their match, they withdraw into watchful quietude.

Individuals are like countries; they must maintain constant vigilance against the possibility of attack. Unless we accept the reality of threats to our personal safety, and the need for occasional aggressive manipulation to insure that safety, we will be as controlled as Czechoslovakia.

Getting Serious

In a goal-oriented society many compete for the same reward. If you ignore this reality, you will fail in your public life, and the consequences will spoil your private life as well. You must clearly differentiate between those people with whom you are competing and those with whom you have private, emotional relationships. It is unwise to confuse the calculating flattery of co-workers with sincere affection. Lasting emotional gratification comes from people who have nothing to gain from manipulating you; professional gratification comes from a goal gained through shrewd manipulation.

If you manipulate for a worthwhile purpose, your integrity and personal relationships will be enriched. If you engage in manipulation for its own sake, you will gradually lose control. One government manager, a noted manipulomaniac, specializes in reorganization. He is constantly revising organization charts and shifting managerial responsibilities, simply for the sense of power it gives him. As we shall see later, in the section on Manipulation Practice, occasional reshuffling can help solidify your position, but pointless rearranging wastes time and goodwill. Chronic manipulators are sick and frequently drop dead before their time.

Uncontrolled emotionalism is also harmful to manipulative situations. Although friendship, enmity, love, and other emotions have a place in our private lives, they do not belong in business relations. The best manipulators are emotion-free. You don't hate a door because it won't open. You examine its latch, its edges, its hinges to see what is wrong. You hurt your toe or fist only if you develop an emotional attitude toward the door.

The same is true of the people and the organizations you manipulate. You look at the characteristics that might help you swing them your way and try to open them up to your control. You hurt your chances of success only if you indulge in the luxury of emotional attitudes toward them.

Anything but logical objectivity in manipulative situations confuses your private life—which should be valuable and pleasurable—with your professional life. You don't score in a team game by playing with private rules. Locate your realistic goals, learn the professional rules, psych out the other players, and win.

Feeling Good about It

Even though "manipulation" has an unpleasant Machiavellian ring, all the executives I have talked to admit to using it. "You've got to live," they say. "It's a dog-eat-dog existence." A romantic rejection of reality does not change the nature of reality. Call it "management," "decision making," or "executive action," you are still talking about manipulation. Business success depends on the ability to view people as objects. Business terms tend to depersonalize, naming a common group characteristic that indicates relationship rather than personality. "Clients," "customers," "patrons," "patients," hint at some special treatment for profit.

Long ago Aristotle made a distinction between public virtues and private ones. Shakespeare too assumed that people should have different value systems for their public and private relationships. When his character Titus Andronicus treats his children as objects and his emperor as a friend, tragedy results. When Henry IV treats his people as objects, he succeeds nicely.

Today the differences between public manipulation and private emotional expression have become obscured, much to the advantage of unscrupulous manipulators. To succeed in private and public life, we need a survival package that gives us a clear understanding of the nature of each.

The virtues of love, trust, and respect can be cultivated in intimate personal relationships because such relationships continue over many shared experiences. A full life includes warm personal interaction, where you can relax your guard and know that you will be loved whatever your faults, trusted no matter how many times you disappoint—a nonjudgmental acceptance like Mother used to make.

These ideal private relationships are harmed when people apply manipulative techniques to personal affairs and subjective emotions to public situations. Apathy and disillusionment are a consequence of this confusion. Only when we distinguish between the private life of emotion and the public life of manipulation can we achieve a meaningful order in either.

Public figures who inveigh against manipulation are only revealing their hypocrisy. Manipulation, used to achieve a worthwhile goal, is not immoral. The immorality is the hypocrisy that tries to obscure reality for personal gain. Sentimental falsification of public relationships and inert submission to the emotional rhetoric of others is far more detrimental than intelligent, goal-directed manipulation.

Winston Churchill would have been a fool not to use every manipulative technique at his disposal to guide England—and the rest of the world—through the horror of World War II. It would be equally foolish for you not to learn manipulative techniques and to know when to use them.

Al the Survivor

Al, a Protestant minister who had moved to Washington and taken an administrative position in a government agency, sat over coffee with me one August afternoon while we talked about the morality of manipulation.

JONES: Would you say that manipulation is ever justified?

AL: If you want to stay alive, it is.

JONES: You have no scruples about using other people for your own advantage? After all, you're supposed to be a religious man.

AL: Religion and manipulation are part of the same life, but everything in that life doesn't have to be the same. I've been used by others at least as many times as I've used them. None of us is much worse off than we would have been unused. The people who bad-mouth manipulation are the ones who don't know how to use it or are trying to cover up their own tricks. We used to have an executive who always talked about his deep religious convictions. He talked so much that we got suspicious. Turns out he was getting kickbacks from one of our contractors.

JONES: You don't feel bad, then, when you treat other people as objects to be managed for your own gain?

AL: Only when I fail. I don't mean to be callous, but I think some of your questions are naive. If people don't enjoy working for a living, maybe they should go into teaching.

JONES: I suppose I deserved that one. I think now you're trying to manipulate me into becoming defensive about my job.

AL: You're quicker than most. Most professors would immediately start talking about how hard they work and how pure their trade is. I know from serving on a college board of trustees that colleges—like all organizations, including the church—are run by manipulation.

JONES: What do you mean?

AL: In every college and university some people want to emphasize research; others want to focus on teaching and public service. Those in control of the budgets are the ones to be persuaded about which direction to move. That "pure" faculty will try any manipulative device to get its own way.

As for the churches? You don't think people just sit around in the College of Cardinals and wait for God to tell them the name of the next pope, do you? They manipulate like crazy. And look at the squabbling between the Episcopalians and Lutherans in America. The more you believe in a certain point of view, the more you're going to manipulate to make yours prevail.

JONES: Your bitterness toward religion could be colored by your own disillusionment with it. Even if what you say is true, do you feel that because everybody does it, that makes it right?

AL: No, but I believe that makes it necessary. I have never done anything grossly illegal, but I have schemed and plotted and bargained as much as I could on several occasions to make sure that the power around me stayed in my control. If I hadn't, you would be talking to somebody else right now. You want to talk to survivors, not corpses.

JONES: But don't you miss the open human contacts you might have with your business associates if you didn't have to manipulate them as impersonal objects?

AL: I'm pretty much a realist. I play cards and golf with them, drink with them, flirt with their wives and daughters, and watch them every minute. The relationships I have are pleasant, though superficial. In my business I don't have time for soul mates. I have a wife and children who love me. With them I am mostly open and trusting. That's about all the openness I can afford.

JONES: You're saying, then, that most of your daily life is at an impersonal level. You've never thought how pleasant it would be to have it otherwise?

AL: You imply a value judgment—that "impersonal" is inferior to "personal." My interactions with my associates are real and satisfying, and I know no pleasure greater than the thrill of a scheme successfully completed. I'd take that rather than a stroll with open conversation any day.

JONES: Then you accept the necessity for manipulation and its consequent depersonalization of human beings?

AL: I not only accept it; I appreciate it. People seem to equate passivity with goodness. The active management of public affairs to achieve a just end is the way the world works.

JONES: But would you admit that to the people you work with?

AL: We don't talk about it. Maybe that's because it's so ingrained. You don't talk about breathing either, but you're doing it all the time.

I have to admit, though, that the word "manipulation" doesn't surface often. Maybe it should. Maybe we ought to come out in the open and talk about ways to manipulate. That could be a new manipulative technique. I've looked at lots of get-successful books, but they're mostly superficial. They don't face up to the reality of power management. Manipulation as we've been talking about it is our breathing process. We can't live without it.

2

PERSONAL MANIPULATION
Controlling Through Individuals

PERSONAL MANIPULATION is control exerted over individuals to achieve a specific purpose, either an aggressive or a defensive one. It occurs in all human relationships, both public and private. Even saying "good morning" to someone is personal manipulation: you expect your action to elicit an anticipated response. If you do not get that response, you are manipulated in turn—to anger, surprise, or some other reaction. Only by being aware of the persistent presence of manipulative situations at the personal level can you control them instead of having them control you.

Every group can be manipulated once you master its personal conventions. Whenever you change environments—whether it is a different town, another country, or a new job—the wisest move is to remain neutral and unemotional until you see the differences between your old patterns of behavior and the new ones. The more experience you have had in observing changes, the quicker you will be able to predict new ones. If you have lived in a closed cultural group, you should not allow any expectations of normal response to color your attitude toward people in the new situation. Wait to see how others respond. Newcomers are always susceptible to personal manipulation because they are unfamiliar with the daily routine.

The classic example of manipulation through cultural ignorance is Shakespeare's Othello, the Moor who came to Venice.
Othello listened to the advice of only one man, Iago, who by
repeatedly saying with candor, "Well, that's the way Vene-
tians act," drove Othello to madness and murder.

In America, where widespread regional differences exist at
the managerial level, it is essential to understand expected
behavior patterns before attempting personal manipulation.
Otherwise your efforts may backfire. When Greg, who had
always worked in a small family business in Mobile, Alabama,
took a job with Dow Chemical in Michigan, his immediate
superior in the accounting department was Ruth, who had put
herself through the University of Minnesota by trapping bea-
ver and selling the pelts to commercial furriers. The first day
Greg and Ruth had coffee together, he stood behind Ruth's
chair to put her into place, following the Southern tradition he
had learned from infancy. Ruth's reaction to his gentility was
red-faced wrath. The action was so artificial and strange to her
that she assumed (1) Greg was treating her like a feeble grand-
mother, (2) he was a blatant apple polisher, and (3) he must
think her an utter fool to fall for such cheap currying of favor.

Since Greg was not blind to the emotional response, he
watched the way others in the coffee shop behaved and
quickly mastered the conventions that made him like the others. Still, Ruth was slow to warm to him because of his initial
error, a perfectly natural part of his behavior that he had never
thought to question.

Individual Types

To avoid the error Greg made in his personal manipulation,
you have to be aware of the possibility of differences in automatic, culture-conditioned responses. Equally important in
personal manipulation is the recognition of major character
types. If Greg had had any experience with regional variations,
he would have seen that Ruth was not of the same breed as his
mother and the Mobile ladies of his youth.

For the purpose of personal manipulation, people can be broken down into three general types: *realists, cynics,* and *idealists.* Those in each group have a specific world view that they believe the rest of the world either agrees with or firmly opposes. They assume the universe is divided into good and evil, with the forces of good—their allies—eternally fighting against the forces of evil—their opponents. Such a grossly oversimplified view of the world is easily manipulated to your advantage. Put aside any idea of educating such simpletons and guide them in their blindness. You will profit from their ignorance without hurting them any more than their own egocentric cosmic view is bound to hurt them.

Most people reveal their basic orientation to life immediately. An inane question such as "Who do you think is the best candidate?" can be the beginning of an intricate manipulation process. The realist will look you in the eye and give you the candidates' voting records or at least quote from their public statements. The cynic will snarl, "What's the difference? They're all crooks!" The idealist will talk about one of them as the savior of the world, the new messiah.

When you know people's view of the world, join them there. It does no good to invite them to join you. You have to take them by the hand and lead them where you want them.

Let's look at how this positive method of guidance works. The ill will of Mr. T, who was several echelons above Ben, would have been a serious handicap. In his opportunities to observe Mr. T at meetings, Ben noted that he was always extremely punctual. Ben concluded, without speaking to Mr. T directly, that he must be a realist. At their group meetings Ben frequently cast a penetrating glance at Mr. T. When Ben made a point, he looked directly at Mr. T, his eyes never wavering.

Mr. T singled Ben out of the crowd as a promising young man. Before long—Mr. T didn't know how it had begun, but he naturally thought he had initiated the practice—Ben and Mr. T greeted each other with a firm, brisk handshake.

As they came to know each other better, Ben cultivated the

habit of using short, terse sentences. He never permitted himself to wander off into tangential considerations or alternative possibilities. Ben knew that the realist's world is one of black and white—slightly more dark than light, but still hopeful. When Mr. T asked Ben to write a report on a conference they had attended, Ben submitted a short document divided into five numbered paragraphs. Ben knew that realists mistrust the fully developed paragraph and can't cope with subtopics. Realists have short attention spans.

Seeing that Ben was Mr. T's kind of man, others began deferring to him. Ben had identified himself with Mr. T's thought process and satisfied it in their relations. Ben became a mirror image of Mr. T in their dealings. When they talked together, Ben occasionally used such unifying phrases as "for us practical people" and "we have to be brutally realistic."

Ben was so successful in seeing the world through Mr. T's realistic eyes that he could present any proposal to Mr. T in terms that Mr. T appreciated. He never stopped watching Mr. T carefully, though, because he knew that realists are not the most dependable types. Their oversimplified view of the universe constantly needs rearranging, so that they shift ground—and allies—with great frequency.

Discovering the general type and working with it, as Ben did with Mr. T, is the positive way to manipulate at the personal level. A negative approach, which is sometimes equally necessary, involves discovering the type and working against it. In another professional situation Ben found himself needing to discredit a realist. Ben saw that Mr. G was a plodder—industrious, diligent, but unimaginative. Ben's quiet questions in public emphasized the man's dullness. Ben tangled Mr. G in intricate discussions of the long-range consequences of any plan Mr. G suggested. Mr. G soon came to be regarded as a hidebound traditionalist, unable to see beyond the present.

When Mr. G presented a suggestion, something direct and honest, Ben chewed on it, twisted it, and flattened it until it seemed ridiculously elementary, the work of a blockhead.

Ben's own language danced and skipped from glittering possibility to shimmering potentiality. Ben's abstract ambiguities made Mr. G's steely eyes cross. When Mr. G tried the direct glance, Ben smiled politely and glanced shyly down.

What Ben did with his realists can also be done with cynics and idealists. If you want a positive response, you mirror their own view of the world. If you need to discredit them, you stand firmly in a different spot.

Cynics, whose distinguishing characteristic is a skeptical negativism, are easily won over. You can enjoy many good laughs with them over the foolish people who still have faith in life. Or, if you want to discredit them, you can suggest that their defeatist thinking will destroy our American way of life. Place your realistically based program for advancement—or your idealistic hopes—against their dark doubts.

With idealists, you can celebrate the virtues of personal emotionalism. You and they know that the true joy of living comes from human relationships. What counts is understanding one another through loyal, cooperative labor. To discredit them, you resort to the realistic argument that sometimes generals have to sacrifice the individual for the higher good. After all, think of the lives that would have been lost if Truman had decided not to drop the bomb.

Identification of these three basic personality types is essential if you expect to succeed at manipulation. And what kind of manager are you? You are none of the above. To be successful, you cannot afford the luxury of a single, undeviating view of the universe. You know that many views exist and you are willing to control them to achieve your purpose. If someone pulls a clever switch on you and you lose your advantage, you can still turn the situation around. Just stay in control of your personal manipulations and pull another switch that puts you out in front again.

The Sheepdog Technique

As you have seen from previous examples, success as a manipulator depends on *attitude control*, the ability to control other people's attitudes toward you, your projects, and your advancement. Knowing what sort of person you are working with is a beginning. From there you move to more specific techniques. Like a good sheepdog, you keep your flock in line. When attitudes are running in the right direction, you run alongside them with a watchful eye for strays. When attitudes stray, you direct them back to the flock.

Attitudes are controlled by reinforcement, redirection, or revision. You reinforce by getting into step and pushing the present attitude. If an attitude conflicts with your purpose, you redirect it by shattering that view and replacing it with a more satisfactory one. Suppose that your proposal is being considered by an important group. Everyone seems satisfied. Then you notice that someone appears ready to move in another direction. Like a sheepdog, you head him off before he can stray to another attitude. Whether it's one person or a group, you anticipate the possible directions of stray attitudes and dog them into your fold.

Revising an attitude is more complicated than reinforcing or redirecting one. Again, like the sheepdog, you do not tremble or bark louder than necessary, because you know you are in control. You can ridicule an opposing attitude out of sight, or rephrase it so that it agrees with yours. With noisily aggressive opponents you assume a gentle, conciliatory tone that shames them into submission. A quiet, rational patience will show them up as towering fools.

Your strongest tool for controlling attitudes is your flexibility. Just as the sheepdog makes broken rushes around the flock to keep the sheep apprehensive and in control, so you present several preliminary attitudes as feints to cover the final rush toward the attitude you want to establish. You begin your manipulative ploy with a powerful, rational argument, surrounded by flip charts, graphs, and data sheets. You are a determined realist, feet firmly planted on visible evidence. When you feel some opposition surfacing, you kick aside the piles of proof, drop the charts on the table, turn off the overhead projector, smile slowly, and become emotional. "All this detail,'' you say dreamily, ''is insignificant compared to the majestical challenge we face.'' With such shifts you control other people's attitudes.

Attitude manipulation is an art, never the same twice. When you have succeeded in shifting the attitude of an individual or a conference group, the people involved are often as appreciative as an audience at the end of a play. They don't applaud, but they look at you with the gratitude of tired sheep safely in their fold at last.

The Yo-Yo Technique

Moods are both a response to attitudes and a cause of attitude shifts. Since people often prefer emotion to facts, *mood control* is of primary importance. In every business situation you should know what mood you want to transmit and never waver from achieving it.

In mood manipulation you should let the yo-yo be your guide. Knowing the final mood you want to achieve, you spin down like a yo-yo to meet opposing moods, but you always come up again to the mood you have decided to create. Perseverence is essential. If others feel that you will surrender to their mood, they will never jump up into your hand. With quiet, polite persistence, you can bring the yo-yo home untangled.

Suppose you are in a conference. It is not to your advantage to have people leave the room in an optimistic frame of mind. The chairman is determined to have an affable meeting. You begin with an effort at responsive laughter, like the others in the group, but it is painful for you. Pretty soon your doomsday mood touches those around you, to whom you have whispered your dreadful thoughts. Your scorn shows through your feeble smile as you respond to the chairman's jokes. When you speak, you fling cold spray on the crackling fire of general jocularity. Gradually, those who have been laughing begin to feel like clowns; and once you control the mood, you control the meeting and its outcome.

As with attitude control, you have to decide whether to reinforce the existing mood or impose your own. Suppose you are going to a superior to ask for clarification of a memo he has sent you. You suspect that when he wrote the memo he was hinting that an important function of your department was being transferred to another. You want a contradiction of that implication. You cannot approach such an encounter in a weak, petitioning mood. If your first statement is "I hope you're not taking this job away from us," you've lost the job. Managers prey upon the weak. They sniff fear as a shark sniffs blood—from far off.

Instead, you join your superior in his mood of quiet confidence. The difference is that your confidence comes from knowing that the job is still yours; others have misunderstood his intention. You and your superior become co-conspirators in an effort to make it as easy as possible on the losing department—the one that misread the memo. You want to help your superior make the other department feel satisfied that the job is remaining where it belongs, with you. If your mood is victorious, you are likely to prevail.

In this scene you are aided by the general observation that managers like to be conciliatory. They don't want people to go away unhappy. You start happy, laugh a little—but not nervously—and then show your superior the letter of explanation you have drafted for his signature. He may want to keep the letter to consider it for a while. That's fine with you. The more he thinks about it and remembers the pleasant mood that surrounded his discussion with you, the more he will be convinced he has made a wise decision. The letter becomes a visible reminder of a bright moment in an otherwise dreary day.

Lighting the Scene

By controlling attitudes and moods—combining the sheepdog and the yo-yo techniques—you can make people see what you want them to see. With careful lighting, you can obscure or highlight the one or two scenes under your control to create an illusory world that suits your needs.

As we have already seen, most people want oversimplified generalizations, a convenient tag for every complex idea or personality. They will tag you, each other, and the universe with catchphrases so that they don't have to think again. This desire for oversimplification is not going to change. If you do not shape people's perceptions, someone else will.

Nearly everyone you know has been given some label: a scoundrel, a drudge, a pusher, an unpredictable genius, or some other equally personality-obscuring phrase. Such stereotyping is probably the result of one encounter or somebody's observation. After the initial marking, any actions that don't fit the stock image become invisible; those that reinforce it are floodlighted. Once you recognize this propensity for falsification through oversimplification, you can use it to your advantage by building the kind of illusion that best suits your purpose.

Chester began his career in the office at about the same time as Dave. Chester was quick to point out the errors his natural competitor made. Chester often spoke of Dave as "the bungler." Within a few months Dave became what Chester had named him. He answered the wrong phone, stumbled over wastebaskets, knocked things off desks. He was the laughing-stock of the office. Chester, by contrast with this bungler, was the fair-haired boy. Such scapegoatism occurs in every group because people need somebody to blame for their troubles. The bungler gives others a feeling of confident unity as they join in thoughtless laughter at his expense.

Suppose, on the defensive side of manipulation, that you are the one being tagged. If you are aware of the way scene lighting works, you already have a certain amount of protection. You cannot defend yourself by refusing to participate in the stereotyping; if you do, you'll be marked as a maverick, an oddball, or a goof-off. The only solution is to set up your own lighting system.

First of all, you have to decide what image you want to project. If you see yourself as the industrious, conscientious sort, turn your floodlight on your desk, with you at it. Some slight rearrangement of your chair and books will emphasize your diligence. Then exaggerate your industriousness. Slightly enlarged work movements, bordering on caricature, will help you create the impression you want. Whenever you walk across a crowded area, you move with purpose and a preoccupied, downward glance. You're never seen empty-handed. You are always carrying an important document somewhere—even if it's only to the coffee room.

If you feel that you would profit more from a "good guy" image, you use a different lighting pattern. You walk across the office with a casual pace, friendly nods, and a wave here and there, even if nobody is there to wave at. Eventually people will say as you pass by, "There goes someone you can trust."

By consciously cultivating a particular image, you protect yourself from the ones others are trying to impose on you. As you begin to fit into your image, it will become an unconscious part of your executive armor. Remember, though, that you must never relinquish your flexibility. When conditions change, be ready with a change of armor. To succeed permanently, the good guy must always be ready to play the bastard when necessary.

In setting up lighting for others, you should not become a bad-mouther. Such blunt action does not influence other people's perceptions and is so obvious that it may mark you as a malcontent. For negative stereotyping, a slight suggestion is enough. "Have you noticed lately . . . ?" you ask, with all the goodwill in the world. Then you focus your lights and let the hint sink in. You don't draw the generalization. You simply find the negative characteristic you want to shine your light on and look for an incident that fits. When you find your single "seed story" and spread it around, listeners and retellers will begin seeing the permanent label shining bright across your victim's face. All you did, of course, was report a single occurrence.

Suppose a colleague has been getting in your way. You watch carefully and notice that he always waits until the last minute to show up at meetings. The second time he comes in after everyone else is seated, you look up and say, "Late again?" After that, it is only a matter of time until you have him slow, sloppy in his scheduling, not on top of things. You have never bad-mouthed him, but you have managed to build an image that will stick with him as long as he works with you.

The ultimate protection against negative stereotyping is direct communication. You can force people to see you as an individual if you spend enough time and effort on the job. Every office has a malcontent; if people start to put a negative image on you, you can always fling the malcontent stereotype back at your detractors so that they are shot with their own gun. One executive saw that the image makers in his department were trying to make him out as a schemer. He cultivated a naive candor that led his associates to say, "We saw right away how false people's bad-mouthing was. What they said just wasn't what we saw at all."

Later on in this book you will learn specific ways of differentiating image types. Right now it is enough to realize that part of personal manipulation is making people see what *you* want them to see, in you and in others. As with many areas of manipulation, you have the choice of acting positively to arrange your own lighting or of doing nothing and being lighted by someone else.

Cooling It

As we have already seen, a good manipulator never confuses professional manipulation with private emotion. In the professional arena friendship, love, even hate, have no place. Emotions destroy the objective detachment necessary for successful control of a professional situation.

Confusing "friendship" with "social occasions" can make

you the manipulatee rather than the manipulator. Sometimes you can make others feel your friendship is honest and true; but if there is something to be gained on either side, you should be cautious. Don't waste time on social occasions that are not enriching your private life or advancing you professionally.

People who act with a purpose are happy, even if what they do seems strange to others. A career executive in Washington was transferred from downtown to the suburbs. He was so devoid of emotions that he said to me, "I have a new wife now who works out here. The one you knew before didn't get transferred, and the car pool got to be such a hassle that I divorced my first wife and married a woman who works out here." The surrender of the personal for the professional is rare, but this Washington executive has no conflicts. His job comfort comes first.

The opposite type, the vulnerable person, is a manipulator's dream. This maladjusted, frustrated spirit expects to find personal gratification in business associations. Phyllis is a good example. She got a job with a public relations firm in Chicago. The three people in her department immediately became jealous of her youth and industry. As seasoned manipulators, they covered their jealousy with friendly overtures. One took her to lunch; the other two introduced her to some of the single men in the office. They gave her a lot of good, honest advice. She prospered and accepted their friendship.

One afternoon, when she said she had a lot to do, they suggested that she take off early. "Nobody will notice," they said.

As soon as she had left, one of the old-timers went to the rule-loving vice-president and told him Phyllis had taken off early. "Watch her," he said, "and let me know if it happens again."

The next week they urged her to take off again. "We'll cover for you if your phone rings," they said in a friendly way. Then they went to the vice-president.

When he called her in the next morning to fire her, Phyllis

protested that the others had told her it would be all right. "You're working for me—not them," he said, not believing what she said. She was obviously a liar trying to shift the blame to others. He was glad to be rid of that kind of employee.

Such friendship stories are common among business executives. Friends are not usually your competitors. You have business acquaintances to manipulate and friends to trust. If you have to have personal support in your social life, seek it outside the office. As you learn to manipulate other people's lives, learn to control your own too, so that you gratify your emotional needs where they do the least harm.

Eating, drinking, and playing with your business associates is a necessary part of your professional life and should not be confused with relaxation. If your associates watch Archie Bunker, you watch him too. If they go to the Chinese place on the corner, even though you hate wonton soup, you'd better go Chinese. If they bowl, fly, or ski, you'll have to make some effort to cultivate your arm, stomach, or legs. It isn't natural not to run with the pack. The recluse who doesn't circulate becomes the "ghost."

It is easy to play this game because everyone wants to be part of a group. Whenever two factions exist—drinkers and nondrinkers, TV viewers and TV scorners—you will have to choose sides for manipulative purposes. Don't make the decision on the basis of personal preference. Make it on the basis of which group promises more for your professional advancement.

Usually you will want to join the ascendant group. At times you may find it more advantageous to join the weaker group so you can quickly become its leader. In that way you cultivate a position of power by determining the "right" place for everyone. Suppose the dominant group eats Chinese lunch. You begin bringing your lunch to the office in a paper bag to eat with the outsiders. Soon the outsiders are the insiders, and those who have been eating Chinese lunch join you for fear they're missing something new.

If people will let you decide where they should eat, they will soon let you decide how they should vote and what they should see in the world. Determining the right personal choices for others is a good psychological boost for manipulators on the way to controlling power.

Humanitarian Manipulation

As you begin to feel the power that personal manipulation gives you, remember to use it gently. Why apply a brutal twist when a tender turn will accomplish your purpose? As you saw earlier in the chapter, desperate, directionless people will be grateful for the security your manipulation provides. For the most part, their gratitude will stimulate a warm feeling or mild affection on your part. This tender feeling for your subjects is not unnatural and should be encouraged, as long as it does not interfere with your ultimate manipulative purpose.

People are constantly falling in love with their physicians, having affairs with their bus drivers, pilots, or stewardesses. Prisoners even fall in love with arresting officers. England has a long tradition of masters who seduce the serving girls they hire. It is all part of the subtle sexual attraction of those in control. Recognize this possibility and enjoy the pleasant by-product of wise manipulation. Be careful, though, not to allow this feeling to make you the manipulatee instead of the manipulator. If you begin to see your tenderness penetrating the surface of your professional shell, remind yourself that it is only your success that makes you attractive, not anything inherent in you. That way you will not sacrifice your success for a transitory emotion.

As long as you put control first in your priority system, you will continue to succeed; you can afford to be gentle, kind, and receptive to the affection that control fosters. If you succumb to illusion in your personal manipulation, your universe will shift; violence and pleasure at inflicting pain—the loser's attitude—will replace the warm glow you feel when you are in control. People in control can even manipulate bitter and resentful associates, knowing how frustrated they must feel. By enduring patiently these losers' cheap cuts and vicious back-stabbing, you will gradually draw these misanthropic people into the security of your control.

Personal manipulation, then, depends on imperturbable calm, which is achieved only through a sincere conviction that you are going to win. And the more you know about manipulative practice, the more secure you become in the sense of your own power. That power is what makes you capable of true humanitarian manipulation.

Personable Paul

Paul survived in an industry where one out of every five executives was fired over a six-month period. He never experienced any job insecurity. He was so certain that he had succeeded as a personal manipulator that he said, "the director and I will be the two people paid to lock the door when they close this place down. And then I'll be hired as caretaker." So far it has not come to that, but Paul is now assigned to head a new recruiting program for executives.

JONES: I gather from what you've been telling me about your career that you feel personal connections are at least as important as natural ability.

PAUL: You better believe it! I've known people with a lot of natural ability who never got off the ground floor.

JONES: Why is that?

PAUL: They don't know how to get along with others. They don't realize how important it is to cultivate people. I don't mean just butter them up, although people need a lot of that too. What I mean is watch them, psych them out, you know.

One of the luckiest things that ever happened to me was having a son the same age as the director's. I came here at rock bottom. I had been a small-town salesman— women's and children's shoes. I never had a day of college in my life and wasn't about to.

Right away I found out the director's son was in another school district; we moved across town so my son could happen to be in his class. I got them both into Little League, same car pool. But I didn't rush things.

We were at a lot of games together, but the director didn't know where I worked until the end of the first season. Was he surprised! He had thought I was a big executive, he said. I told him I'd learned a lot about people by fitting them for shoes, but I was handicapped in business because I had no formal education. He probably had no idea how much snobbish prejudice there was right in his own shop.

I played up the self-made-man bit because I knew he'd come from a disadvantaged home himself. He decided I shouldn't be kept down. Without my knowing it— so I wouldn't be embarrassed—he had the company offer me a job in public relations. I built a whole department to work with the community. We had a budget of half a million just to interrelate. Then I took over in-house training as well. Now I'm personnel director for the whole shooting match.

JONES: You may be fooling yourself. Maybe it's your natural ability that got you where you are. You obviously have a lot of it, or you wouldn't have made it this far. You're not doing justice to your own talent.

PAUL: Talent, hell! I've seen too many people with talent get the ax. I've had Ph.D.s crying on my desk when I broke the termination news to them. They're the talented ones. I've just got plain old pull.

Jones: Maybe you're right, but aren't there a lot of people around here who resent your influence?

PAUL: Of course. I don't work here to be liked. I manage all the emotions—hatred, fear, love. That's what I learned selling shoes. You slip on the shoe you have in stock and talk the customer into thinking it fits. That's the way I work the personnel in this old place.

I've doubled efficiency around here in my time. I've got lots of charts and graphs to prove it. I just talk people into it—sweet or sour, whichever it takes. I know they laugh at me, but they're also aware that I've built myself an empire that overshadows the whole plant. If they closed this one up tomorrow, the director and I would probably be off for the West Coast to run one there.

JONES: So you can manage other people's actions and emotions, cope with jealousy and backstabbing, and still enjoy life. How do you do it?

PAUL: You've got to have confidence in yourself. You've got to know that you can control. If you think you can, you can. I may not win them all, but the more I win the better my chances of going on winning.

I fish a lot—with the director and his son, you know. And sometimes when we're playing a slippery perch, the director says, "You're as gentle and as sure with that fish as you are with department managers."

That's the way I do it. I know the kind of fish I'm working with and how to land it. I don't try to pull in a trout and a catfish the same way. Get the point?

JONES: You mean you treat people like fish?

PAUL: Something like that. You know what you want to catch and you do it right. But you still remind yourself that it's just a game. That way you never take it too seriously. I can always go back to selling shoes. That keeps me from running scared the way some of these creeps do.

JONES: You don't have a lot of respect for most executives' intelligence, do you?

PAUL: I know some are pretty smart, but not in every way. I watch to see what they want to see, and then I arrange myself in a world that they're looking for. I answer their dreams for them by reflecting just what they know the world is like. Then they think I'm a great guy.

JONES: You think that personal control is the most important aspect of business life?

PAUL: You can say that again, buddy. You can sure say that again.

3

ORGANIZATIONAL MANIPULATION
Controlling Through Structures

ORGANIZATIONS are composed of individuals, but at times it is more convenient to manipulate the organizational structure than the individual people in it. Earl, a hospital administrator, was aware that in every hospital tension exists between physicians and fiscal officers. Without considering the personalities of the people involved, Earl set the two groups against each other like gamecocks. He watched the feud sap the strength of both sides and then took over a controlling position with the hospital board. Before the struggle was over, both the fiscal officers and the physicians were grateful to Earl for working to clear up the ill will that he had—without their knowledge—cultivated from the beginning for his own advancement.

Earl achieved his administrative success only by continuous sensitive observation of his organization. Successful manipulators learn to observe corporate structures as well as individuals. Whether people are working for IBM or a three-man shop, they regard organizational patterns as sacred, something to be feared and worshiped. From that reverence you can often take your cue for manipulation.

Efficient, foresighted executives see the organization as only another object to be manipulated. They make their organization a temporary shelter for their professional lives, shaping it to their immediate needs and then moving on. Executives who expect to find consistency, beauty, order, or purpose in an organizational structure are going to be not only disappointed but victimized by those who know better.

Elting E. Morison, in his book *Men, Machines, and Modern Times,* tells of the time-motion expert who discovered that gun crews in World War II had two members who did nothing but stand at attention during firing. Their presence was a carryover from cavalry days, when two men had been detailed to hold the horses of the men who were firing. Until the efficiency expert analyzed the situation, no one had wondered about the two extra members of each gun crew. They had just always been there.

Such outmoded patterns abound in every working unit. Change is effected slowly—and someone always benefits from it when it comes. Two generations of farmers sold chickens to stores throughout Missouri. The third generation became millionaires when they realized they didn't have to sell the chickens alive. They cooked them, packaged several pieces in frozen-food containers—along with dressing, peas, and potatoes—and marketed them to the stores that had once bought their live chickens. Other chicken farmers in the same neighborhood are still selling eggs door to door.

People who are not intimidated by organizational intricacy will be able to manipulate the system for their own purpose. As always, realistic observation is the place to begin organizational manipulation.

Vanishing Power

You can observe structural possibilities easier if you are not observed observing. Information about other departments, patterns of behavior, the power structure, must be accumulated unobtrusively. You maintain invisibility by asking few questions and listening carefully—not snooping around, but reading everything that comes your way.

When no one is watching you, study the published information provided by your organization. It will not reveal the real organization, but it will show you the public image the present power shapers want to project. From this illusory structure you can begin to explore the actual one.

The actual and the illusory intermingle, even in the minds of the power shapers. The ones at the top may have come to believe their public image; such executives are open to manipulation through organizational propaganda. At lower levels most of the executives have come to accept the public image without questioning its authenticity; its rules and purposes govern their lives. You can manipulate these executives by talking to them in terms of the structure they perceive. From the official manual and board reports you learn the right vocabulary, the accepted pattern of perception. Unless you think and act in accepted terms, you will be unnecessarily— dangerously—visible.

No one must know that you are beginning to see the actual under the illusory. Don't let personal delight or ego gratification tempt you to lay aside your cloak of invisibility. Ego is the enemy of manipulators. A small dose of it produces instant, uncontrolled visibility, which undermines the observation process.

Owen was a new interviewer in an industry that hired seasonal labor. In his department the summers were frantic, but during the winter the work slacked off. After a year in the job he began to see the seasonal pattern and, in a moment when he felt that he was not receiving enough attention, pointed out how slack the period from December to June usually was. "Why don't you transfer some of the work from another department to our department?" he asked at a staff meeting. "Then you won't have so much wasted time."

The managers, who had been unaware of the slack in their personnel office, looked at Owen for the first time. He became, visibly, the slack that he had reported. Examining the organizational structure, they discovered that December to June was a frantic time in the fiscal department, where year-end reports had to be prepared. Alert to the need for flexibility and interdepartmental cooperation, they decided to shift office positions to take care of the slack time in the two departments.

Under the new arrangement, a few people from the fiscal office came over to the personnel office after their rush was over in June. With the increased efficiency in the two offices, management was able to cut personnel; and the most recently hired employees, including Owen, were let off. Not many people were surprised to see Owen go, because he had violated one of the cardinal rules of organizational manipulation: remain invisible unless you have a long-range purpose for surfacing.

Any emotional need for attention, favor, or personal gratification may thwart your attempts at organizational manipulation. At times you will have to surface temporarily; but most of the time you should see more than you are seen. Wrapped in invisibility, you can observe structural tensions and flaws that will crack open at your touch and give you a clear passage to success.

One young executive, quietly searching through the company's past records, found that an executive training fund established in 1910 had been inadvertently omitted from the budget for the past 20 years. The endowment in the fund had grown so large that when he applied for it he had enough for a year's study in Switzerland. The experience and contacts he gained that year were invaluable when he returned, happily visible, as one of his company's major executives.

Permanent invisibility, you see, is not necessary. Early in your career you will need to be seen once in a while, but you should know when you are being seen so that you can control your visibility-invisibility power. When you become visible, choose your time wisely. Psychologically, mornings are the best time for running around the halls and hopping departments. People are rested then and are not pressured to finish the day's work. Don't hang around, though. Simply pop in and make some casual comment. Over the months people will begin to remember you as a pleasant face. Gradually, they will begin to tell you what they are working on. Soon you will have a good understanding of how people in different parts of the organization spend their time.

Unnecessary visibility is always a liability. If you talk too much to too many people, you will gain a reputation as a nuisance. The only time you want to be visibly connected with irritation is when you are fomenting dissension. In such cases you must make sure that the irritation becomes focused not on you individually but on the organization, which is exploiting everyone. You visit other departments and make casual comments: "My section is unbearable. I have to get away once in a while." Before long people will begin to tell you how things are going in their departments, and you will have a sense of the total organizational mood.

Once you gain control of your visibility, you can make sure that you are seen when promotions are at hand, when committee assignments are handed out, and when someone is being sought for an assignment that might lead to advancement. Then you don't mind being noticed.

You achieve visibility or invisibility as your purpose demands it. Without self-consciousness, you hold your breath and sink into obscurity. You find yourself quite naturally at the backs of groups; your face is always bent over your desk; your clothes blend with their surroundings. You are as well camouflaged as a rattlesnake on the prairie.

When you consider your sterling qualities, your infinite cleverness, you naturally stand out in a crowd. You move with such grace and elegance that people around the water fountain whisper to each other, "That's a person to watch."

Cloud Watching

Your organization is like a white cloud on a windy spring day, reshaped by every breath that stirs. You can never say "This is the way it works." All you can say is "This is the way it has worked the last few times." Every change of officer, board member, or secretary influences how it functions.

Those who think of the structure as a solid building rather than a formless cloud are handicapped from the beginning. If you accept its inconstant state, you will be able to collect enough information to stir the breath of wind you need to shape the organization to your purpose.

You can collect your data through oral statements, printed information, and comparison and contrast. The first two sources are useful only insofar as they reveal the attitudes of their authors and assist you in drawing comparisons. They should be evaluated carefully, with attention to the speaker or writer's motive for presenting them.

Organizations, like individuals, have complex personalities. They can be understood only by comparing them with others. If you know only one person, you will assume that person is the way "people" are supposed to be. When you come to know a variety of people, you can begin classifying them according to types. Then you learn to spot individual strengths and weaknesses. As with people, so with organizations: comparison is the aim of your cloud watching.

As you talk to people who have worked in other places and read executive descriptions of your organization's structure, you can begin to construct your own generalizations. You discover that your organization is not a single, isolated entity, but part of a national complex. As you hear catchwords like "accountability," "flexibility," and "responsibility" in national news broadcasts, you find that your co-workers are using the same terms.

Your organization's response to the national mood guides you to the correct manipulative procedure. If yours is a conservative, independent-minded organization, when the nation cries "accountability" you can argue that you have always maintained a high degree of accountability and point out that you have been running program evaluations for the last ten years; or you can argue that the idea is a fad that only upstarts will heed. If, on the other hand, your organization is ambitious and swinging, you can quickly design a program that shows your alertness to current trends, your responsiveness to innovative ideas.

The information you collect about your organization, other organizations, and the national scene is raw material for shaping your success. Anything you know may contribute to a wise professional decision. But the collecting job is never complete. The spring winds keep blowing that billowing organizational cloud across the sky, and you have to watch the changing shape constantly if you are going to control it.

Committee Crosstrumping

Organizations operate by a combination of administrative action and committee decision. Individual executives have certain controlling powers, but the impersonal will of committees is at least as instrumental in effecting change. Personal manipulation can lead an executive to decide in your favor, but an easier way, sometimes, is to manipulate the organization through committee behavior.

Participation on committees, subcommittees, planning groups—any small group involved in decision making—gives you a chance to manipulate the organization. Again you use comparison and contrast, but in a different way. By working on several committees, you can use information derived from one to impress the members of the other.

This technique, known as "crosstrumping," gives you a chance to instill cooperation in the groups you work with. Soon you will become the organizer, looked to by others for efficient and rapid change. Actually, what you are doing is multiplying committee activity to give the impression of control; and passive members of the committees will believe you have it.

On the committees you want to become either the chairman or the secretary. In these positions you have control of the action. As chairman your shaping powers are those of the preparer; as secretary, those of the recorder.

Suppose you are the chairman. In preparing the agenda, you

can omit items likely to be detrimental to your point of view. If you are forced to include them, you put them at the end of the meeting. You allow other members to dwell on insignificant matters so that troublesome questions are hastily handled when everyone is tired. Anyone with committee experience knows that issues debated during the last half-hour are never examined thoroughly. Knowing a committee, you can pass or destroy a plan by the place you give it in the agenda.

If you are the secretary, your power lies in the written word. You are responsible for the minutes. If the chairman has spent an hour on a favorite issue, you can reduce the discussion to a single sentence, split between the bottom of one page and the top of the next. Anyone reading the minutes is likely to over-look it completely. Or you can bury the chairman's point in the middle of a long paragraph with a quotation in it. Nobody reads long paragraphs or quotations.

As secretary, you can control the meeting itself by carefully interrupting the discussion to destroy the train of thought. You ask for clarification in such a way as to throw doubt on the chairman's integrity. With an innocent smile you suggest by your questions that the chairman is trying to put something over on the committee.

If a secretary becomes an antagonist in this way and you are the chairman, you can save yourself by bringing your own secretary to take minutes. Or, to bury them completely, you can suggest that the proceedings be transcribed from a tape of the session. That way, the minutes become so massive as to be inaccessible.

Whether you are chairman or secretary, the principle to re-member is *control.* You can control the present as chairman, shaping the agenda or the discussion, cutting off opposition, encouraging supporters. As secretary, you control the past and the future by the way you write the minutes of the meeting.

A committee member can also manipulate the proceedings. As a concerned participant, you bring in a flip chart or handout for your part in the discussion. Since nobody else on the committee has given any thought to it, you will so impress the others that they will be easily managed.

I recently watched Doug achieve his purpose by a technique known as *committee threat.* Knowing that all but one or two members of the committee were apathetic, he sent around a notice saying that if he did not hear any negative comment, he would assume the committee members endorsed the action described in the memo. In that way, he concluded, the committee could avoid time-consuming meetings.

When two of the five committee members sent back notes expressing doubts about the proposal, Doug asked his secretary to call each one and say that the majority of the committee was in favor of the action; they would have to call a new meeting to give the opposing members a chance to state their objections.

The secretary called the first dissenter and asked him to prepare his arguments for committee presentation.

"Let me talk to Doug," the committee member said.

"I'm sorry, but he's away right now," the secretary said, following Doug's instructions.

"Oh, hell! I'm not going to go to the trouble to face the committee about this," the executive said. "Tell Doug to forget about my note."

The secretary played the same game with the second committee member, with the same results. If Doug had called the meeting, he would have probably lost out to these two active participants; but the threat of a meeting was enough to carry his point. Asking people to put time and effort in to back up their position is an effective way of manipulating the organization.

As a committee member you can sometimes force action— or delay it—by suggesting a series of meetings. By threatening to prolong a committee's deliberations, even for a few weeks, you can usually get your action approved. On the other hand, if someone else is trying the threat, you can insist on a series of meetings and wear the others out by delay tactics.

If you don't have the time to spend on meetings, you can resort to the *democratic ploy*. Every organization pays lip service to the democratic process. When you are crossed on a committee, you can allude darkly to "fascist tactics," "suppressive measures," or "communist authoritarianism." Whatever rhetoric you use, you should be convinced that the organization is not living up to its fine American heritage.

When you tire of nationalistic rhetoric, you can adopt the moral-outrage approach, consciously using emotional, judgmental words to sway others. You suggest that undesirable actions are "immoral," "ethically dangerous," or "morally appalling." Such terms mark you as a watchdog of corporate virtue.

Don't fall prey to your own rhetoric, though. One major executive who began with the moral-outrage approach became so convinced that his organization was immoral that he resigned from the company. Your rhetoric should not becloud your clarity of purpose. If you keep your initial purpose firmly in mind, you will have no trouble playing out your hand—and your crosstrumping will win the game for you.

Phone Fun

The telephone is the nervous system of the organization. The phonebook and the phone are essential tools for an eager manipulator. The office directory gives you a clue to who is on top. In some directories the major offices are listed separately; in others they are included in the general listing. Such arrangements suggest whether the mood of your organization is autocratic or democratic.

The office directory was put together by someone who has been around a long time. Its pattern tells you a lot about the true structure of your organization. Are secretaries listed with some officers and not with others? Are some departments omitted? Study the book in the light of what else you know, and you will learn a great deal about your organization.

The phone too is a valuable manipulative tool. It can answer your questions if you know how to ask them. You first call someone you know to find out who knows the answer to your question. Sometimes you make a dozen calls, but you finally come to the person with the answer. Your time has not been wasted, because you now know new people who may be useful to you in the future.

Here's an example of how the phone facilitates organizational manipulation. Elmer wanted to find a cheap convention center for a weekend meeting, so he called a friend in another department. "Oh, yes," his friend said, "we have a good place for meetings. I don't know what the arrangements are, but you can call Ted Deering."

From Ted, Elmer discovered that the vice-president's office made arrangements for meetings. When Elmer called there, the secretary said, "The board always meets there. Mr. Deering was there originally, I think, as a guest of Dr. Rutter, a friend of the president."

Elmer now knew about the convention center. He also knew Ted Deering had access through Dr. Rutter to the president of the board. Thus Elmer was on his way to seeing how friendships and organizational structure interrelate.

Phone systems tell you where the action is. A zealous new manager has a more sophisticated phone system installed right away. The president has a conference system installed, and the pattern spreads. A new long-distance system suggests new corporate relationships. The prosperous, favored departments have whatever telephone luxuries the phone company is pushing.

As each system becomes commonplace, though, chic departments discard it. When real estate hawkers and magazine salesmen start using long-distance calls, the upper regions rediscover the value of letter writing. When the lowly and insecure start aping their betters with telephone conferences, superiors install a closed-circuit television system for conference use.

Phone practices are a clue to where organizational power

lies. Just be sure you don't draw any hasty conclusions from any one piece of information. If a manager answers his own phone, he may not be important enough to have a secretary; or, as is true in some large organizations, he may be important enough to have a direct line of his own. Either the manager *has* to answer his own phone or he *chooses* to answer his own phone.

Similarly, if you have to go through two secretaries, you may be dealing with a well-protected person or with someone buried in the organizational bureaucracy. If you are trying to reach someone who is always in conference, the executive may be busy, inefficient, or on the golf course. If you have to make an appointment to talk on the phone, the manager is probably an eager organizer—but that is all you know. Never take action on the basis of a single piece of data that can be interpreted in two ways.

Obtain supporting information before you chart your subject's exact power position.

Skillful manipulators develop their own telephone style. To show how busy they are, they hold a phone to their ear while they greet a visitor with a warm handshake and a helpless shrug. When the phone rings with someone in the office, a manager may let it ring with some such comment as "Let the bastard wait. I'd rather talk to you."

Displays of phone power demonstrate a person's value to the organization. Some executives tell their secretaries, as they usher a visitor into their office, "I'm not here unless the director calls." The fact that the director hasn't ever called doesn't keep them from making the statement. Of course, such poses are retold with amusement by secretaries at coffee.

A *favorable phone balance* can tell you how you and others stand in the organization. Unlike the nation's trade balance, you should have much more coming in than going out. When your phone stops ringing, you'd better start dialing to remind people that you are still around.

Tinkertoy Time

Even in a conservative organization you will have opportunities to make changes. The change may be a minor rewording of job descriptions, a revision of personnel practice, or a slight adjustment of personnel policy. Whatever it is, make the most of it.

To gain power, you usually have to shake up the present power system. If your manipulation is not proceeding as well as you'd like, suggest that you be put in charge of some minor revision. Nobody else will want the job or notice that it is being done. If you make the adjustment effectively, your opponents won't notice the loss of power until their phones stop ringing.

Otto, for example, knew that most of the other department heads took time off after Christmas. He arranged to have the bylaws changed so that the budget approval was moved from June to January. That meant that department heads had to stay home for last-minute negotiating or let someone else handle it. The first year the new system was adopted, Otto's budget increased 15 percent more than those of competing departments.

As a member of the traffic committee you can initiate a change in working hours to avoid traffic congestion. Not until after it goes into effect does anyone but you realize what it does to your opponents with school-age children and working spouses. Or, you can make a gradual revision of job descriptions so that more people with your professional orientation are hired. Over the years you will build up a position of power by organizing a clique of your own. Such minor changes in structure can shape your organization to your liking and give you that needed feeling of survival.

People who see through the chaos of organization obscurity are likely to be in control. Some persistent, though indistinguishable, pattern keeps organizations running in spite of endless incompetence and stupidity. By addressing yourself to that chaotic confusion and imposing your own Tinkertoy pattern on part of the organization, you will prevail.

If you have a chance to serve as a consultant for other organizations, grab the opportunity. There you can see other manipulators at work, people who will talk freely to you because you are an unthreatening outsider. With candor they will reveal to you, as they have done so often with me, the small patterns of order that have gained them great managerial power. You can study their techniques and implement them in your organization so that your Tinkertoy tower is such an essential part of your organization that anyone who destroys you will destroy the organization itself. Your system is probably no worse than the chaos it replaces, and this one has a bomb-proof position for you.

Organizational Perception

You have to have multiple vision to perceive the organization in all its manifestations. Even though the shape of the organization is constantly shifting, you must work with each situation as if it were the permanent one. The same is true of your position in the organization. It is at once fluid and seemingly permanent. You have to know where you are at each moment, but you must also remember that fluidity is the nature of organizations. Nothing stands still. Things shift for no visible reason.

Don't let the formlessness of corporate structures upset your manipulative plans. Optimistic glee should be your attitude toward the shifting. Whenever you are in a corner, remember the corner can soon become a vantage point for a leap ahead. At such times you should view your organization as a massive ice flow as well as a cloud bank. The only fatal error is to continue to stand still in the same spot; as long as you jump from one chunk of ice to the next you'll probably stay afloat in the icy corporate river.

As you can see from the suggestions offered in this chapter, you will probably never find a foolproof scheme for managing your organization permanently. Your major consolation is that no one else will either. Take every piece of data you have and work with the hypothesis of the moment as if it were a permanent solution. Be ready, at the same time, to revise your hypothesis when a new piece of information comes along.

Joel the Job Hopper

Joel has held seven positions in the past three years, all within the same industrial complex. Joel has increased his budgetary control from nothing to over $5 million and has been responsible for widespread organizational restructuring.

JONES: Elliott Richardson is the only person I know who has done more job hopping than you. What do you gain by these moves?

JOEL: An understanding of the organization I work for.

JONES: Does that help the organization?

JOEL: Not immediately, maybe, but I think that what helps me helps the organization too.

JONES: Could you expand on that point?

JOEL: I'm learning to manage power. Whatever I learn about control will make me a more desirable manager. My expertise will benefit the company.

JONES: Do you feel a commitment, then, to this one company? If you got a better offer from another one would you remain with this one, your first teacher?

JOEL: Probably not. Right now I feel a total commitment to this company; it's the one I'm giving my life to. If I had a better offer from a major competitor, I'd shift my total commitment to that company.

I see your cynical smile, but what you don't understand is that even then what I've learned with this company will help both me and this company. It's naive to assume that big business and big government don't have the same aim. Wherever I am, what I have learned about management will indirectly help all the companies I've worked for.

JONES: So you view companies as you would view a group of individuals; you see them as competitive but also interdependent. Is that right?

JOEL: Yes. I think that's a good way of looking at American organizations. Every company admires the people who can best understand and negotiate within its complexity.

JONES: Would you say that personal gain is your major motive?

JOEL: Isn't it everyone's? I'd do anything I could get by with to gain more power.

JONES: As you've moved from position to position over these past few years, have you found that most people have the same motivation?

JOEL: I think so. The ones who survive, anyway. They're very realistic about what they are doing to get ahead.

JONES: You mean they're going to have to learn how to manipulate their organization for their advancement?

JOEL: That's what I mean.

JONES: If you were advising someone else about manipulating the organization, what would your first piece of advice be?

JOEL: To learn as much about the real location of power as possible and to struggle to get as much of it as possible as soon as possible. When I first started here, everyone described my job as a "minor administrative position with no future." The people who had held it before me had retired. That didn't bother me, because I saw right away that my office would put me into daily contact with the people who handled budgetary decisions. I grabbed control of personnel and budget and made a major program out of something stagnant. I called new committees and restructured the entire program.

JONES: Did that improve the program?

JOEL: No, the program was adequate as it was. But it certainly improved my career. I went to all the national meetings I could and met executives who could teach me how to play with power. I got an idea from them about another program and suggested it. I got approval and became manager of a new department.

I gathered all those I knew who were hungrier than I was and put them in charge so that the reports from my department would reflect our great success. By handing out pitiful budgetary crumbs I built up a lot of goodwill. Then my old friends saw that I was a grabber and decided to use me as their bright young front man to obtain federal funds. I talked the standard liberal line and began making the Washington circuit as a lobbyist and fund raiser.

Meanwhile, I saw that a big budget of my own was the only way to permanent power. When I came back to the home office, I worked out a reorganization scheme that got me small budgets that had been held by others. They didn't know the budgets were gone until I was writing checks on their accounts.

JONES: You don't feel that you have to maintain goodwill with all your associates, then?

JOEL: Only with those whose help I need. It's ridiculous to think that the people you manipulate out of a budget are going to love you. But you hand control to someone who will be subservient to you—and grateful too. The others you keep down with talk of their incompetence, their bitterness, their self-seeking. That's what I've learned from observation, and it's worked for me.

JONES: What do you see as your future?

JOEL: I enjoy what I'm doing. I expect to work myself into a board position so that I can have the final say about the way the company goes.

JONES: Do you think you know where it should go?

JONES: I think I know as well as anyone else. And I'm not as foolish as some of the old fogeys I've conned. I don't think there's any one corporate destiny. I'll be damn good, though, because I know that American business is simply a reflection of America itself. If I know about organizational structures, I also know about government structures. And, knowing that, I can come close to international control by the time I'm 55.

JONES: That's quite a dream. You really believe that organizational manipulation runs the world?

JOEL: Of course. I've seen enough to know that the person who controls the structure controls the power. And I like power.

Manipulation
Practice

4

FLATTERY

Greasing the Skids

FLATTERY is the simplest form of personal manipulation. The wife cheers the husband on; the mother encourages the child; one friend praises another. Psychologists classify flattery as a form of positive reinforcement. When people do what you want, you reward them with kind words, gentle looks, and admiring responses. Positive reinforcement can be used at any level. As you develop skill with flattery, you can sense how much reinforcement to give people to maintain the right BS balance for them.

The usual rule is that the more insecure people are—in themselves or their position—the more reinforcement they can absorb. Beginning secretaries, for example, perform better with a few words of praise after every task. One executive told me he doubled his secretary's daily output when he consciously began praising her speed and efficiency.

By whatever name you call it—"morale building," "encouragement," or "blarney"—flattery builds goodwill. To be an effective tool for manipulation, however, it has to be consciously controlled. It cannot become an automatic response to every situation. Like all powerful tools, flattery, used carelessly, harms the user. People who hand out random compliments soon gain a name for insincerity and are not trusted for anything they say.

Injecting the Grease

To succeed as a flatterer, you must measure your doses with such accuracy that your recipients compliment you on your perception and probity. Don't give the next injection until you see the patient begin to sag. Then inject an unexpected surprise that sends the blood rushing through his veins again.

I have observed many skillful flatterers at work and have discovered that their pattern consists of three relatively intricate steps. With practice, skilled flatterers learn to recognize symptoms of overdosage and go inactive while they wait for a more appropriate occasion to continue their grease job.

STEP 1: ESTABLISHING DOSAGES   The three personality types discussed in the chapter on personal manipulation—realist, cynic, and idealist—require very different doses of flattery. Cynics need the largest dose because they are deeply afflicted with self-doubt. Their universe is a bitter one, and they have probably never received enough loving. You should administer your flattery in small, frequent amounts and increase it regularly until you get some positive reaction—"Oh, cut out the bull," or "Do you really think so?" Then decrease the dosage momentarily but keep the flattery bottle handy.

Realists require only moderate doses. Their suspicions about the world make them alert to the possibility of flattery. For this reason, special techniques such as reverse flattery discussed later in the chapter are especially suitable for realists. Since realists are sometimes allergic, the first dose can be fatal to future flattery relations if it is not carefully administered. Once realists have identified the medicine you are using, they'll reject the medication in the future.

Idealists, sensitive spirits that they are, require only light medication. A few milligrams of gentle flattery give them a high for a week. Because they hold such a high opinion of themselves and the world, it takes only a few kind words to reinforce what they already know to be true: they and the world are on the verge of becoming what they deserve to be—perfect in every way.

Whatever the personality type, the right dosage will bring your subject around. Mrs. Ashe was so cynical and alienated that the 17 people working under her quivered fearfully whenever they were called into her office. When Cora was transferred to the department, she was filled in on her superior's vile personality. The last two people in Cora's position had been fired because of that hellhound, Mrs. Ashe.

When Cora heard what she had to contend with, she was unperturbed. "I know the type," she said quietly and closed her ears to the horror stories the others were anxious to unload on her. Realizing that Mrs. Ashe was a career woman who had made it in a largely masculine society, Cora was immediately sympathetic to the sacrifices the woman had obviously made for her career. No wonder she was bitterly cynical.

Cora began her flattery manipulation in the best possible way. She identified with Mrs. Ashe and honestly saw the world from her point of view. In that way she sensitized herself to the appropriate dosage. The first time Mrs. Ashe stormed at her, Cora stormed back and stomped out of Mrs. Ashe's office. Cora waited a few minutes, collected her emotions, then went back in. She gave Mrs. Ashe a story about how tension-producing it was to exist in a world dominated by men. It was only natural for women to react sharply; what Cora admired about Mrs. Ashe from the first was her refusal to let the bad qualities of men sully her relationships.

"That's all right," Mrs. Ashe said, totally reconciled. "I probably have let masculine brutality affect me over the years, just the way you did this morning. It's unavoidable in our job, but we can be efficient without absorbing men's weaknesses. I'll help you all I can."

From that moment, Mrs. Ashe and Cora ran the office. Strangely enough, Cora's continued flattery about women being able to do a better, kinder job than men made working conditions more pleasant for everyone. At the Christmas party

Mrs. Ashe sat beaming in the midst of her convivial workers. She had always scorned the parties in the past. "I don't know what's happened to Mrs. Ashe in the last year," somebody said to Cora.

Cora showed the good sense that all flatterers must have when offered an opportunity to show their hand. "I don't know either," she said, "but I've always found her very pleasant to work for." Cora's dosage was successful because Cora selected it carefully and administered it secretly.

STEP 2: MONITORING THE PATIENT   Establishing the adequate dosage is only part of the flattery job. Flatterers are on 24-hour call. They must monitor the patient and remain alert to changes.

The adequately adjusted patient poses a different problem from the inadequately adjusted one. After the Christmas party Cora had to change her flattery pattern. Any reference she made to the plight of women in business would have reminded Mrs. Ashe of her wretched years and turned her quickly against Cora. Mrs. Ashe's potential for cynicism continued in her personality, making her suspicious of those who might throw her back into a black mood.

At the first sign of change Cora dropped her old medication and found a new one. For Mrs. Ashe the new year brought a new Cora too. In the next stage of their relationship Cora was slightly less aggressive with her flattery. Now that the social adjustment had been made, Cora could go about her job and flatter Mrs. Ashe with nothing more than an occasional admiring glance or pleasant word. An expression of gratitude was the minimal dosage that kept Mrs. Ashe and Cora on friendly terms.

Flatterers should always guard against overdosage. A large part of effective flattery is quiet observation. As you will see later in the chapter, your major duty is to watch your patients. By listening to what they say and what others say about them, you learn when to give reinforcement and when to remain passively in the background. Most people are pleased with any attention but they don't like to feel supervised or shadowed. Give them just enough attention to achieve the flattery level you need. That way you can be sure of the well-greased skids —the purpose of flattery for manipulators.

STEP 3: MAKING THE PATIENT MOVE   Once you have mastered the first two steps in the flatterer's art, you are ready to bring out behavior patterns that are dormant in your subject. One psychology class used nonverbal flattery during a semester to condition their professor so that he spent most of his time walking about with his hand stuck into his shirt front. By an agreed-on signal, they leaned forward and listened more intently whenever he brought his hand up to his chest. By the end of the semester he lectured most of the time in a Napoleonic pose.

Although your patients may be smarter than this psychology professor, the techniques for moving them are the same. You do not create new behavior in your subjects; you simply develop what is latent in their personalities. Flattery is filling in the blanks, not writing a new essay.

To get your subjects to behave as you want, give them admiration and approval whenever they display the slightest tendency toward favoring you. If you have spotted what they want and established the right dosage, you can gradually cultivate the desired behavior.

Be careful at this point, though, that you have not misdiagnosed. Symptoms can sometimes be contradictory. As we saw earlier, people's stated attitudes often differ from their real attitudes.

Nick was certain that he could flatter his boss by praising his shrewdness in budgetary matters. Unknown to Nick, the boss paid a great deal of attention to budgeting, not because he thought it was important but because he hated it and felt ill at ease with a balance sheet. Nick's constant praise of a painful area of the boss's professional life caused the boss to develop an undefined antagonism toward Nick. Thinking that he was not being flattering enough, Nick increased the dosage—only to find that the boss became more antagonistic. Eventually he cut off all communication with Nick.

You make your patient move in the direction you want by applying minimum pressure in the right place at the right time. At the slightest indication of withdrawal or uncontrolled jumping, return to your desk and begin at "Go" again. Only then can you be sure your flattery will not backfire. As you will see later in the chapter, the art of flattery has many subtle variations; until you know all of them you must use this powerful manipulative tool with care.

A Light Buttering: Personal Flattery

When Willie Loman, the salesman in *Death of a Salesman*, tries to show interest in his boss's family, he fails pitifully because he has no understanding of the boss or his family. Successful personal flattery should be lightly intimate and sincere. Clichés and superficiality ring false at the personal level, where success depends on intimate knowledge of your subject.

Unless you are willing to spend the time developing this intimacy, the light personal touch is not for you. Once you start your file clerk talking about his love life, he will use you as a cheap psychiatrist. With subordinates, you have to make it clear from the beginning that you are interested in their personal affairs but are also quite busy. When they initiate a conversation at your desk, pick up some papers or reach for the phone. That way you are in control of the flattering situation.

Time and place are important for effective personal flattery. Some people feel threatened or confused when personal subjects are broached in a professional situation. Don't try personal flattery when people are at their desks, the center of their public lives. Neutral ground such as hallways, elevators, and restrooms are good places to get in a quick personal punch.

Coffee shops, candy counters, and barbershops are places for more prolonged butterings. At those times, when your subject is moving between the personal world and the public one, you can serve as a useful transition figure, making the psychic transfer from home to office—or the opposite—more pleasant.

Experienced flatterers collect personal data mentally for use at an appropriate time and place. Less experienced ones resort to note cards with names and ages of spouses, children, sick mothers. If you don't care enough about your subjects to keep up with their private lives, you had better leave personal buttering alone. You can destroy the goodwill you have built up by asking about a child who's been on hard drugs or a spouse who ran away with the tour guide last summer.

You don't need to restrict your interest to pleasant subjects. People like to talk about their troubles as well as their successes. When you listen to your manipulatee recount a wretched tale, be sympathetic but objective. Don't condemn anyone involved, even when the narrator indicates a hatred for his wife or mother-in-law. The runaway wife may return tomorrow, and you don't want to be remembered as one of those who maligned her.

In *therapeutic flattery* of this sort your job is to provide encouraging examples. Three other executives' spouses have left them, and look at the happy results. Society is responsible for the druggie, and look how many kids have experimented and are now straight, working in banks and industry.

You cannot rush the relationship that paves the way to personal flattery. Your subjects must think they have initiated the openness that permits them to unburden themselves to you, to brag to you. Your stance might be called one of aggressive reticence. You are there, available, but not eagerly interested at first. Maybe you sow a ''seed story'' from your personal life. If the object of your flattery responds positively, return to the same idea later.

Suppose you mention that you are going bowling after work. A blank stare or an artificial smile and you never mention bowling again. "I bowl too" and you bring up your score the next time you see your manipulatee. When your subject begins telling you his scores, where he bowls, and what kind of ball he uses, you have opened up the personal area for flattery purposes.

The same technique works for family flattery. You mention your wife's sickness, and you get a disinterested nod or a complete diagnosis from personal experience with sick wives.

Older executives often like to relive their youth through younger associates. They may become greedy to hear about your wife's pregnancy, her threatened miscarriage, her desire to work outside the home. An old man who has become too successful to take time off for fishing will give you every detail of a fishing trip he made 20 years ago.

Feed these people just enough of your personal experience to initiate a response. Skillful flatterers don't get butter on their sleeves. You are cultivating your subject's self-love, not expressing your own. When you start talking about personal experiences, be sure you are doing it for your subject, not yourself. If you keep your purpose firmly in mind, the flattered one will come back for another light coating of butter— whether you are listening or talking. Nobody gets enough personal attention.

Personal appearance is a good area for initial flattery. Suppose you are one of many people in an outer office. When your superior passes your desk, you give him a casual glance. After a few days, you turn and follow him with your eyes as he passes. One day you get up enough courage to say to him as he goes by, "Can you tell me where you get your hair cut? I'd like to get mine cut there too."

For both sexes, haircuts are a matter of great concern. Maybe your boss will blush and say that it's a trade secret. Even if he does, he'll be flattered by your attention. He will probably tell you, though. After that, the barber becomes a common subject for conversation between the two of you. The barber will also supply you with a wealth of personal information about your subject. You and the barber may even become co-conspirators in an investigation of your boss's personality.

Here again, though, you must not rush the personal flattery. Your subjects must believe that your interest is sincere; if that illusion is shattered, their response turns to loathing—for themselves for having been duped by a flatterer and for you for having debased them with verbal manipulation. The best way to avoid such a danger is to be really interested in people. That way, your flattery is gradually transformed into genuine concern. Flattery, well used, can lead to close personal relationships and thus lose the name of flattery.

A Heavy Grease Job: Professional Flattery

Since professional flattery does not require establishing a close relationship with your subjects, it can be spread on much thicker than personal flattery. You and your subjects share the values of the same professional world. You sometimes have to make them aware, though, of how much alike you are. At some point in the grease job someone may say, "We're really a lot alike, aren't we?" With some degree of surprise—and a lot of relief—you agree. You know now that you've been training the grease gun on the right spot.

Unless you begin by establishing this sense of shared professional values, your flattery will not count for much. If your subjects are old-line conservative and you are new-breed liberal, your admiration may make them wonder if they are standing up for the things they believe in. Study their professional aims and reflect them back.

Remember, though, that what your subjects say professionally and what they actually believe may be quite different. They too are trying to stay afloat in the system. As you are working on them, they may be giving somebody else a grease job. You can find out your subjects' actual beliefs, as opposed to their publicly professed ones, by what newspapers they read, who their favorite columnists are, and what TV shows they watch. One Washington executive employs a Ph.D. full time to summarize articles in the papers and journals his superiors read. You may not need to go that far; but if your subjects read *U.S. News and World Report,* you should be familiar with its attitudes and editorial policy.

It is not difficult to find the source of someone's professional pride. People see the world in terms of their own strengths and weaknesses. Their strengths are the characteristics they notice and praise in others. Their weaknesses are the qualities they disparage in others or regard as insignificant.

Carson prided himself on his tolerance of diverse points of view. After taking a course from an ivy-league liberal in the 1950s, he continued to demonstrate his understanding of neo-Marxist principles. The young executives around him soon found counterculture rhetoric an effective flattering device. One well-enunciated "bullshit" could endear a young hopeful to Carson more readily than a month of drudgery.

By listening to your subject's favorite phrases you develop a rhetoric of effective flattery. Professional pride is revealed as much in how people speak as in what they say. Here are some verbal indicators of current popular areas of professional pride.

Enlightenment. People who use the word "enlightenment" are in superficial revolt against their background. They retain their original behavior patterns, but they enjoy mouthing the shocking revolutionary thoughts of those who withdrew from the executive game. You must not mistake what these people say for serious criticism of the system. They are bound to it by strong emotional and financial bonds. You develop the easy rhetoric of revolution, but you do your work and support the status quo.

Competence. People who favor the word "competence"— and related terms such as "thorough," "skillful," "technologically sound," and "reliable"—are the drudges. They follow the party line slavishly, have few original ideas, and have pushed ahead by sheer hard work. They take stuffed briefcases home every night and write long reports with many subdivisions. They are difficult to work with because they like to have their own values reinforced and need constant reassurance that they are more than competent.

To play to their self-love, you mimic their behavior—stuffed briefcase, furrowed brow, and long hours—but once in a while you introduce into the conversation an idea that cuts through the red tape and gives life and fire to the drudgery. You treat the idea, the moment of lucidity, as if it were their own. Never display originality as yours; let your overflowing creativity water their parched souls anonymously. Then praise them for creative competence, for their amazing combination of hard work and genuine originality.

Shrewdness. People who use the term "shrewdness" frequently see themselves as hard-nosed realists. They are easy to manage because they are the most gullible of the lot. They bluster, rant, and pound the table, but they are pushovers for a sob story. They have a wide streak of sentimentality. Since reality is so complex, they have no consistent policy and will be swayed by your subjective approach to the world.

Give them a strong dose of reinforcement. Admire their strength of character and uncompromising adherence to practical experience, and play them with the emotional bait they long for. Realists, who are sometimes less educated than others at their level, are trying to hide their insecurity among theorists and abstract thinkers by emphasizing the importance of the practical. Agree with them; ask them for advice and encourage them to generalize and philosophize. People tied to the concrete, as we have seen, enjoy broad, unsupported generalizations.

Excellence and accountability. Smug, superior types with lots of assurance emphasize the need for developing excellence and accountability—establishing evaluative processes to weed out the deadwood. They obviously don't think they are part of the deadwood; or, if they do, they believe that by talking fast and getting on the team they can establish an evaluation procedure that is sure to put them well out in front.

With people of this breed you must play the snob game. Let them know you set your own standards high, and show them how uncompromising you are with mediocrity. Because of their smugness, they need almost constant reassurance. Their self-centered universe cannot tolerate the slightest hint that they are not perfect. They are the only group of flattery subjects with an infinite capacity for praise. No matter how much you gush about their professional superiority, they will never suspect that you don't mean it. You are only saying what they believe. Any reserve on your part will be taken as lukewarm support. For the accountability crowd, bring out your rococo special.

Creativity. People who hate detail work—the broad-brush types—like to be known for their creativity. They also need to be admired as good guys. They can be manipulated by praise for their fuzzy-headed schemes. They think of themselves as jolly opponents of the drab; their purpose is to bring new light into the dark establishment.

Unlike the smug, superior breed, these people are not so sure they are right. Charts and statistical tables intimidate them. Still, near the top of their priority list are the personal relationships that obscure professional responsibilities. One of their favorite terms is "human being." Tell them that they are genuine human beings, and they glow with fulfillment.

These creative types are mavericks, nonconformists. They have to be handled carefully because they are emotional and develop lasting grudges easily. You cannot trust them far because their allegiances fluctuate with their mood. They can turn upon you even while you flatter them because the crosswind of their creative subjectivism has caused them to veer suddenly in another direction.

Collegiality. The word "collegiality," now making the rounds with the "in" set, is a sign of the brutish mass mind at its worst. Derived from the word "colleague," it originally referred to the professional community. As it is now being used by those of an uncreative, authoritarian bent, it has come to mean conformity to *my* way of thinking.

People who use this word are dictators who will brook no deviation from absolute righteousness. They are insecure types who cringe in fear when they are met head on. They are the most difficult to flatter because it takes a strong stomach to endure their professional arrogance. Since they want conformity, your only recourse is to make your actions agree with their plan for the universe. They despise all authority except their own and pour scornful wrath on the incompetence of their superiors. Unless you are a member of their mutual-admiration society, you will have to play a servile Uriah Heep, rubbing your hands and smiling. It is usually wiser to try some other form of manipulation on these people because flattery is so distasteful when directed at them.

With all these groups, pride is the key to flattery. People who do not have professional pride are grease-proof. But most people are proud of some aspect of their work, even if it is how much they get by with. Through their language, then, you can find the right way to shoot them full of heavy professional grease. Just make sure you don't overdo the grease job.

Grease Rationing

As you learn more about the manipulative uses of flattery, you begin to see it as a long-term project. Although you may occasionally let your natural instinct to flatter take over, you should always have a definite purpose: control of the flattered person, not just for the moment of flattery, but for the entire relationship. You must ration your grease over a long period.

Lowell was such a successful flatterer that his co-workers could recognize and name his techniques. He operated so systematically that his friends called him—with admiration in their voices—"the slide-rule hypocrite." Lowell began by evaluating the influence his subject might have on his career. Then he analyzed various ways to get physically and emotionally close to his subject. This proximity firmly established, Lowell built a relationship directly related in complexity to the amount of good the flattered person could do him.

He never worked with one flattery job at a time but wove

them together into intricate *cross-flattery*. He would rarely praise anyone directly. He would tell one subject how much he had respected another's behavior in committee. Thus the flattery, transmitted through other mouths, took on an aura of truth. The implication was that Lowell was so straightforward that he could not ingratiate himself the way others did.

Over a long period such secondhand flattery was extremely effective. Lowell spread the word among his subjects that he knew how much they distrusted flattery, but that left him unable to show how much he truly admired them. This approach clearly suggested that the subjects were immune to the flattery the common herd lapped up.

As part of his long-range program, Lowell also used *reverse flattery*. He occasionally uttered a blunt and telling criticism, hedged with positive reinforcement. Such directness cleared him even further from being identified with sycophants. Constant attention to the strength of the entire mix was part of Lowell's success in the grease-rationing business.

Like Lowell, every flatterer needs to establish a time–reward ratio. Careless flatterers may become the manipulatees unless they ration carefully. If you loiter over coffee, permitting yourself to be drawn out about family affairs or your job, you are not using your time or your relationships efficiently.

The biggest danger in the flattery relationship is jealousy. A proficient flatterer refrains from public praise, not just because it is in bad taste but also because it can create jealousy among those being flattered. A sensitivity to relationships will help you suppress any jealousy that arises among those being flattered.

Jealousy, once recognized, can become part of the flatterer's game. Jake wanted to flatter Mr. Stone to improve their relationship. Quite by accident, he mentioned the name "Harold" in conversation one day. He thought that he saw Mr. Stone wince slightly at the name. Jake went back to the office directory and looked up Harolds. He found one at the same general managerial level as his boss. Quietly, by questioning secretaries and old-timers, he discovered that a terrible feud existed between Mr. Stone and Harold; whenever Mr. Stone and Harold got together they ended up shouting at each other.

Jake decided to use *contrast flattery* with Mr. Stone—a dangerous, daredevil variety with high emotional stakes. The next time Jake had an opportunity, he compared the smooth operation of their section with the chaotic lack of discipline and order in Harold's section. He did not mention Harold by name, but referred only to the section.

Mr. Stone's response was immediate. "Have you noticed that too?"

"I don't know why the two sections are different," Jake replied. "The only thing I can assume is that it must be the personalities of the two managers."

"That's right." Then Mr. Stone unloaded on the trouble with Harold's section. It was Harold.

After this initial exchange, Jake became a constant supporter for Mr. Stone. Together they excoriated Harold's actions; Jake contributed rich new legends about Harold's incompetence to Mr. Stone's already sizable collection. This bond of common hatred, one of the strongest unions in managerial circles, drew Jake right up the executive ladder. Flattery, you see, is made as easily out of hatred as out of self-love.

Another danger in flattery—an almost unavoidable consequence of it—is disgust. Somewhere along the line flatterers are filled with disgust for themselves and the people they are flattering. They despise the subject for gobbling up the sweet talk they are handing out.

When such dark moments come, a realistic appraisal of necessity is the only remedy. Most business relationships are dry and unrewarding. Flattery is the grease that keeps bureaucratic machinery running. Without flattery numerous executives might collapse under the weight of tension and self-doubt. The flatterer is a benefactor to humankind, spreading assurance and confidence among the incompetent and stupid.

If such positive reinforcement does not help, flatterers can always go home and wash the grease out of their throats with a bottle of whisky. If that cleansing agent fails, flatterers can run themselves through a reality session, talking freely to spouses and families about how they really feel. By blasting the subject of their flattery in private, flatterers can retain the bland and affable smile that costs so much to maintain in public.

Kevin, King of the Grease Monkeys

Kevin was in the difficult position of having three bosses. He reported to the president, but he was also subordinate to a vice-president and an executive fiscal officer. The three had totally different personalities. The president was conservative, bigoted, rough-hewn. The vice-president was polished, well educated, progressive. The fiscal officer just wanted his accounts to balance.

JONES: Have you found flattery a useful tool in executive management?

KEVIN: No question! One of the finest.

JONES: With so many people to report to, how do you keep a consistent flattery pattern going among them?

KEVIN: That's part of the fun. I've had these three guys doing just what I want for three years now.

JONES: With flattery?

KEVIN: Right! When I talk to each man, I put myself in his position. I can do that because I know them each so well. The president got me a place in his club. We go there with our wives. He drinks a lot and talks freely. With the vice-president I got tickets to the symphony series. I see the budget officer at work every day. So, you see, I have a chance to be alone with each one of them. It's important to see them alone at times you can count on. That way you can make your plans ahead of time.

JONES: But it wasn't always that way. Before you had a reason to see them privately, how did you manage?

KEVIN: I always had a feeling when I needed to talk to one of them. I kept in pretty close touch with their secretaries so that I'd know when a crisis was developing. Then I'd stop in with an article I thought they would like to see, or some information I'd been meaning to bring around. I didn't make a pest of myself, but I was a face they were glad to see and confide in. I brought them the reassurance they needed when things were tough. That's the way I got in with them.

JONES: But they're so different. How can you be in agreement with all three?

KEVIN: I saw right away that a power struggle was going on between the president and the vice-president. I played to that. I'd spend a lot of time telling the president how dangerous it was to have people around who didn't believe in the old values. Then I'd go to the VP and before long, as I listened to him, I'd be sympathizing with him for having to work with that old stick-in-the-mud. The budget officer, of course, was in between, the way I was. He was grateful for any tidbits I'd bring him about the others. He just wanted peace.

JONES: But didn't the two compare notes on you?

KEVIN: Sure. The president naturally assumed that I had to get along with the VP. The VP was the same. When I'd tell one of them how I'd conned the other one, he'd laugh and laugh. We'd laugh together.

　　　Each of them knew for sure that I had to keep up appearances with the other one. And I'd share information I got when I was with the other. They came to use me as a go-between when they wanted to transmit information. I'd sometimes say to one of them, "Are you telling me that because you want me to know it or because you want me to tell it?" That was always good for another laugh.

JONES: And what did you expect to gain from such obvious double dealing?

KEVIN: Promotions, raises, preferments·of all sorts. Both of these men hate each other, and the fiscal officer is scared all the time. I'm safe, though. Whoever wins, I'm going to be right on top. If the VP gets the ax, I'm next in line. The president loves me. If I thought I could swing it, I'd mount a campaign to slander the VP out of office. But I'm not sure enough yet, so I snuggle up to him at concerts.

JONES: Does your wife approve of your attitude toward your work?

KEVIN: Sure. She backs me all the way. We sit at home nights planning what we're going to say. You see, if I tell the president something one week, my wife tells his wife something to support it the next week. That way it has the ring of ancient truth, especially if it's about how shrewdly the old boy has nipped some innovation in the bud. Then we both commiserate with the VP and his wife about how stodgy the other two are. My wife is a valuable flattery reinforcer.

JONES: Do you ever feel disgusted by your duplicity?

KEVIN: We both do, my wife and I. I come home pretty bilious after some of the stuff I hand out, but we start talking about how smug and stupid the guys are when they fall for that bullshit, and pretty soon I'm all right again. Anyway, we've gained so much that we don't mind the dirty feeling. You can be dirty and unsuccessful or dirty and successful.

JONES: You haven't said much about the fiscal officer.

KEVIN: He's probably the easiest to flatter. He is so scared all I have to do is tell him that the president said a good word about his department and he loves me for a year. I practice on him. When I look over one of his reports and rave a little, he feels great. He doesn't believe half of what I say, but he likes to hear it anyway. So many people give him hell that a kind word goes a long way with him. He laps it up, even when he's telling me it's bunk.

JONES: Do you think anybody flatters you?

KEVIN: Plenty of people. And they'd better too. Flattery goes with my job description. I encourage it as much as possible. People who are worth flattering have power in other people's eyes. And you don't really have to have power. It's mostly illusory. What you have to have is a few people who think you're important. Then you are. And the flattery keeps coming to make the illusion real.

5

DECEPTION

Muddying the Waters

Although extremely creative flatterers may approach the complexity of deception, deceptionists need more skill than flatterers to sustain their illusions. To succeed at deception, manipulators must build a verbal screen around their subjects to shield them from anything that disagrees with the desired illusion.

The word "deceptionist" should not be confused with the more commonly used word "deceiver." Manipulation by deception requires a high degree of finesse. A deceiver is someone who knowingly sets out to delude people. A deceptionist is a manipulator who has raised illusion making to its highest level. Deceivers may be insignificant, self-seeking immoralists. Deceptionists are polished, cultivated practitioners of an ancient and noble art. Their deceit may be for gain, but gain of such proportion that a special word is needed to describe those who pursue it.

A deceptionist's view of reality must never waver. If you get caught up in your own deception, you will be destroyed. Cyril, for example, set out to create the illusion that he was an extremely sought-after executive. He asked his friends in other companies to send him letters inquiring about his interest in top-level positions with their companies. His secretary left the letters around so that prying rivals could see them by accident. At his own expense Cyril made several trips to Washington, ostensibly to serve as special consultant for big business.

By the end of his second year of deception Cyril had come to believe that his organization could not survive without him. In a conversation with the president he said, "If you don't go along with me on this, I'm going to accept one of the offers I've been getting."

The president looked at him with an amused smile and said, "That would be a good idea. Why don't you?"

When Cyril wrote his friends who had collaborated on the deception, they had no openings for anyone at his level—or at any level. They thought he had understood that from the beginning. He had better stay where he was; times were hard.

After six months of unemployment Cyril, frightened and filled with hatred, was the only person who still believed the illusion he had created. He could not understand how someone with his managerial skills could be unemployed.

Deceptionists weave their illusions on the twigs of a cool control of reality. The illusions are no stronger than those twigs. Since deception is usually practiced on superiors, deceptionists must always keep in mind their true place in the power structure.

Some deceptionists, thrilled by their early success at stirring up mud, forget the intelligence of their subjects. By underestimating their quarry, they suffer significant professional damage. Future deceptions are difficult to initiate once the deluded person sees who's got the muddy stick in his hand.

These warnings, though, should not discourage you from engaging in deception. You are as smart as the people you are playing against. Otherwise, you would not still be playing. As long as you retain a firm grip on reality, respect the intelligence of your subject, and keep your illusion under control, you will be a skillful deceptionist.

Illusion Shopping

We shape our view of the world out of the patterns of behavior we perceive around us. Most of these patterns are so subtle and varied that we are not conscious of them. Shrewd deceptionists see them as raw material to be refined for their own products. They shape illusion out of the actuality they observe; and if that illusion is successful, it creates a new actuality. Then deceptionists are no longer deceptionists. They are prophets who saw the shape of things to come and worked with them to hasten their arrival.

The present contains infinite possibilities for the future. By emphasizing certain aspects of the present and deemphasizing others, prophet-deceptionists control the future to their own advantage. Orville looked around his office to see what the future might hold for him. He saw five other executives of his own age and rank with equal or better qualifications for their jobs. He knew that if he was going to do more than survive he would have to create an illusion that he was in some way special. His problem was to find the right illusion to cultivate for his particular managerial situation.

He knew that he should shop carefully before buying the illusion he wanted because an illusion that doesn't fit can cause a lot of pain. He had to have an illusion that would please his superiors without alerting his competitors to his aggressive game. If he were obviously a sycophant, the Eager Young Thing, neither his colleagues nor his superiors would find him attractive. No. That illusion was too close to stark reality to be palatable to anyone, including Orville. Eager Young Things were as old-fashioned as Horatio Alger.

He also discarded the possibility of creating an illusion that he was a carbon copy of his superiors. They had gotten where they were either by influential contacts or by hard work and dogged determination. One of Orville's colleagues had once bragged that he was related to the Du Ponts, but his illusion was so ludicrously self-serving that it offended rather than helped.

Putting aside these possibilities, Orville looked around for something that would make him unique, an illusion that would raise him above the ordinary workers and get him visibility at promotion time. Rummaging through his past, he remembered that he had been editor of the school paper when he was in the ninth grade. He had always enjoyed editing work because it was so easy—a comma here, a dash there, a corrected misspelling, and you were ready for the press.

That ninth-grade assignment was one of the last times that Orville had thought he was important. He knew that good illusions begin with re-creating a sense of self-worth. When you feel important, you are less susceptible to vague fears; you are less likely to posture and brag as insecure people do.

So Orville took his special talent for editing out of memory storage and applied it to the present. He bought himself a thick blue editing pencil and read over the last office report. He found three misspelled words, two misplaced commas, and a split infinitive. He circled these errors in his copy and diffidently approached the superior who had control over the report. ''I don't want to bother you, sir, but I've had quite a bit of editing experience and I wonder if reports should go out of our office in this condition.'' He placed the blue-penciled copy on the manager's desk and stood quietly while the man read it.

After this event, Orville was marked out as ''the guy with the blue pencil.'' He was an editor with special knowledge. He knew how the written language should look. The other managers at his level, and those above him, began to bring him their letters, send their secretaries to him to ask about style, and consult him about their outlines for technical reports. Within a year everyone in the organization accepted Orville as the ultimate authority on the written language. In two years he was writing the president's speeches and soon became special presidential assistant.

Orville still keeps his blue pencil in the top drawer of his walnut-and-chrome desk, but he doesn't use it much. He doesn't have to, since the illusion he created has become a reality.

When you make others believe that you are a creative, successful person, you are not so much creating an illusion as underlining one side of your intricate personality. As we saw in the discussion on lighting the scene, skilled manipulators display events so that they read the way they want them to. They study someone's present view of reality and then warp it slightly so that it leans toward the illusion to be perpetrated. Good deceptions do not twist reality so much as they build on it.

Illusion shoppers must be careful not to misinterpret reality. Charlie and Dave were new in their organization; both planned to advance by deception. Each, unknown to the other, was trying to shape his boss's view of the world so that he would favor him. Charlie studied the boss carefully and saw that he was an easygoing realist who wanted people around him to be happy. He went to some trouble to maintain a reasonably friction-free atmosphere. Seeing this characteristic in his boss, Charlie classified him correctly as an optimistic realist.

Charlie also analyzed his competitor. Dave was a strong pusher who would do anything to get ahead. Charlie's conclusion: he would reinforce the boss's present world view and let Dave dig his own grave. Thus Charlie became a part of the optimistic, good-hearted, friction-free environment. In spite of Dave's nasty remarks, Charlie remained jovial and friendly. When he talked to the boss and others about Dave, he had nothing but praise for him—only he wished Dave were happier in his work.

Dave didn't bother to analyze present personalities. He decided to mark Charlie as a goof-off because that was the way he perceived Charlie's friendly demeanor. Vigorously, Dave began calling him "Good Time Charlie." He worked hard himself and snarled at Charlie's effortless progress.

In a few months Dave thought it was time to destroy Charlie, so he brought a charge of incompetence to the boss. The
boss's response: ''You've been a troublemaker ever since you
came. If you can't learn to work more smoothly with other
people, you'll have to find another job.''

Dave had made the mistake of building his illusion against
existing facts. Charlie, more wisely, had seen the most easily
created illusion and worked with that one. If the boss had been
bitter and cynical, Dave's choice might have been the right
one. It is not safe to assume that good guys always win. They
win only when they have a place in the dominant pattern. The
discordant element in an existing world view is likely to get the
ax.

Bill, for example, believed in a solid set of virtues. He began
work for an employer whose life had been devoted to skillful
deception, a mood reflected in his department. During the first
month Bill had to report gross misuse of the computer terminal
and the Xerox machines. The employer thanked him for the
information and sent out memos on the correct uses of equipment. On several other occasions Bill called the boss's attention to personnel incompetence and made suggestions for improved efficiency.

In spite of his honest efforts, Bill didn't fit in. When he
spoke at staff meetings, the employer snarled at him. Bill
didn't know what the trouble was, but at promotion time he
was overlooked. Within a year Bill had to look for another job.

Bill's trouble was that he was not a deceptionist at all. He
could not shape reality to suit his own purpose. Instead, he
tried to impose his world view on the environment and thus
antagonized his employer.

The world view from which deceptionists draw their raw
material is constantly shifting. A new personality, a new regulation, can change the mood of an office or an entire industry.
When the deceleration of space research began in the late
1960s, optimism disappeared from heavy industry. Jokes and
laughter were replaced by gloom and fear. Anyone trying to

retain the old attitude looked like a clown at a funeral. Wise deceptionists move with these inevitable currents. They take the prevailing view of reality and shift it only enough to suit their manipulative plans.

Rolling Your Own Dream

Occasionally these slight readjustments of reality are not enough for your purpose. You have to create a completely new illusion, one that speaks to your subject's unsatisfied longings. Like a good con artist, you prey on people's weaknesses and create the illusion that their secret desires are being fulfilled. Your illusion promises them a position of power, the money they've always wanted, the friend or lover that they saw portrayed in the movies of their adolescent years. With a little effort you can substitute a treasured dream for the illusion under which your subjects are currently working.

The illusion you create does not have to be a positive one, of course. Your purpose is sometimes better served by creating a nightmare instead of a dream. Most people are sure that somebody else is really out to get them. While others are plotting their destruction, you are trying to help them. As you cut off other lines of communication, your subjects become more and more dependent on the details you provide. You isolate your subjects from all other views of reality. Their minds become a blank screen on which to show the illusion you have selected.

Subject isolation is useful whether you are building a positive or negative illusion, because it is easier to work independent of conflicting views. You can invalidate other influences by pouring in so much support for your own illusion that the other pictures are blotted out.

Rob, who wanted his boss to hire one of his friends, began shaping his illusion six months before a vacant position opened up. Rob alluded frequently to the imbalance in hiring. Too many engineers had been hired from the same school. Employment statistics showed that the best companies had employees with diversified educational backgrounds. Rob found articles to prove that point and left them on his boss's desk. When the position became vacant, all Rob had to do was point out his buddy's unique training. The man was hired.

Two years later Rob wanted to get an old college friend a job in his department. This time he cultivated the idea that industry had discovered how important it is to form a critical mass of integrated minds. An action group should comprise at least three specialists with the same research background. When the new position opened up, the boss saw right away that the wise move was to hire a man of Rob's choice. The three friends became a powerful pressure group that imposed its will on the rest of the department.

Rob's success illustrates how illusions are shaped. The manipulator finds a subject's secret desire and plays to it. Rob's boss was convinced that he could build a fine working staff— something almost every conscientious boss wants. Once Rob saw the persistence of the boss's dream, he provided data that would point the way to satisfying it. Since all the information was slanted so that it would also fulfill Rob's plan of getting his friends in with him, the boss and Rob were both satisfied. Nobody lost, except those who opposed Rob.

One of Rob's strengths was the fact that he began cultivating the new illusion long before he could be accused of self-interest. As decision-making time drew near, the manipulator grew silent and let his already prepared illusion work for him. Foresighted people like Rob can do a lot with illusions.

Another thing to notice in this example—something even experienced illusionists are often surprised about—is the shortness of corporate memory regarding illusions. The more complex an organization, the shorter the professional memories of the people in it. In a simple engineering shop Rob could not have manipulated in seemingly opposite directions over such a short period of time. In his busy shop, with everyone preoccupied with frantic activity over a two-year period, people quickly forgot that it was Rob who had argued for diversity of training previously.

In shaping his new plan, Rob was not changing the illusion itself, after all. He was still speaking to his boss's hope of making a great working team. With published articles to support his point, Rob was cooperating both times in the effort to make his boss's illusion into a reality. Even if the boss had noticed Rob's change, Rob could have pled that he had been mistaken the first time around; he now saw more clearly what it took to make a viable working unit.

I have seen operators on state university campuses work the same way. One year they are arguing hysterically for better undergraduate teaching. The next year they are saying that anyone can teach undergraduates; what they need is a highly visible, prestigious graduate program. In both cases their goal is to squeeze money out of the legislature for another fiscal period.

Working Models

As we have seen, the best illusions are built on observed reality. Most executives want to believe at least one of the following illusions. With minimum deception you can work in one of these fake worlds to serve your own purpose.

Organizational Efficiency   The idea of an efficient working unit is dear to the hearts of most managers. To cater to this illusion, you show your unique role as a member of an efficient working team. You are goal-oriented and project-centered. You point out that the entire Western world has benefited from progress. Darwinian evolution is the model for the success of efficiency: the best survive.

Rob appealed to efficiency to get his friends into his company. Orville proved his uniqueness within the efficiency illusion by becoming the final authority on the written word. The tendency to stereotype in organizations will trap you unless you use it to fit yourself into a position of esteem. Most members of the team are regarded as worker bees. As such, they have no particular talent and can be replaced at any time. Active manipulators must show that they contribute something to group efficiency that no one else can offer.

To prove yourself valuable, you must find out where your skills can be most wisely exploited. Do not feel that you are not something special. You are; all you need to do is to find your specialty and cultivate it within your group. Each organization has its own idea about what constitutes efficiency. If your company is big on long hours, you can point out that efficiency is not drudgery but skill; then contrast your own quickness with the time-server's slowness. If your organization is big on specialized tasks, you can become the generalist who has the overall picture that the specialists can't perceive because of their short-term view of management. Whatever approach you take, remember that you are something special. As long as you accept this fact humbly you will be a nonexpendable item in an efficiently run organization.

CREATIVE EXCELLENCE   Opposed to the efficiency world view is the excellence view. According to this approach, creative minds don't work in teams, but in constructive solitude. Like mathematicians at the forefront of their discipline, they are building with such genius that they do not yet have a vocabulary to express their findings. Managers who believe in creative excellence are elitists at heart. They believe that they are superior to the organization. Play to their egos and you build their dream world.

The ego needs of excellence managers vary, of course, with their personalities. Usually, though, if they talk the excellence game they are desperately afraid they have not made the excellence team. You need to talk a personal approach with these executives, making them feel they can relax with you and not have to be out in the field proving themselves. You give them constant compliments on their professional attainments and make them feel that you share their goals. To that extent, your deception dovetails with flattery to form a two-pronged assault. You like them immensely; they can't help liking you in return.

Louis saw that Mr. S was totally committed to the illusion of excellence. He knew that few people in his organization could achieve Mr. S's standards, but the ones who did were the ones to be rewarded. Louis also saw that Mr. S needed someone to define excellence for him. Louis devised a list of the characteristics necessary to achieve ex ·llence. He derived these from prestigious sources: ivy-league business journals, editorials from *The Wall Street Journal*, and handbooks from government agencies. Naturally, the list coincided with Louis's own outstanding characteristics. Mr. S accepted Louis's model as the forerunner of the perfect organization that the elitists would form when they had retired and transferred all the drones.

THE I-CENTERED UNIVERSE   Closely akin to the elitists are those who believe that the world rotates on their axis. Their world can be built out of their ambition, their lust, or any other sin you wish to trot out. Make them sex objects, with all the women in the organization yearning for their bodies. They'll believe it. Make them the one person the world can't get along without. They're waiting for you to notice what they already know.

The distinguishing feature of people who labor under the I-centered illusion is the narrowness of their vision. Unlike the elitists, who are firmly convinced that they and a few others are specially talented administrators, I-centered people refuse to believe in the excellence of anyone but themselves. They have the burden of running the entire organization. Their conversation is full of comments like "I don't know what they'd do around here without me; I'm the only person who cares." Alert yourself to the distinguishing "only's" in their conversation and you'll spot the I-centered types easily.

You cannot join these people in their effort to achieve excellence because they scorn you and everyone else. All you can do is become a contributor to their egocentric existence, a groupie following their rock show. They will accept your adulation and believe the wonderful things you tell them.

If I-centered subjects are in a position of importance, you may run into competition. Others will be playing the same flattery game. To distinguish yourself from the pack, you will have to offer your subjects a special illusion tailored to their secret narcissistic desires. Since they enjoy looking at their own image in a mirror, give them a mirror that reflects their secret yearning to be totally appreciated. Let your eyes be the only place where they can find true understanding and admiration. You can do it, because everyone secretly longs for sympathetic understanding.

THE INQUISITION FIXATION   Many people are waiting for you to assure them that someone is out to get them. You should have no trouble fostering that illusion, especially if antagonistic groups already exist in your organization. Let the paranoid types know that you are trying to help them, but the Grand Inquisitor is waiting for a chance to get them on the rack. For many melancholy souls the world of hatred and persecution is a very real hell. Do your bit to encourage their apocalyptic vision.

As with all illusions, you must not push too hard. When people see persecution just around the corner, you are likely to be suspected of being an agent for the opposition if you take an active role in stirring up your victims. Paranoid types respond best to sympathetic listening. An occasional reminder when they calm down is all you need to keep the illusion functioning to your advantage.

Watson discovered that Mr. Foster, his boss, had a secret fear that someone was going to bring a malpractice suit against him. No malpractice suit had ever been filed in their industry, but Mr. Foster was extremely fearful of litigation. He knew that if he got into the courts he wouldn't have a penny left, and sooner or later they always get you into courts.

Whenever Watson wanted a slight change in procedure for his department, he suggested to Mr. Foster that the secretaries might file a discrimination charge against him or that he might be caught on a breach of contract if he didn't come through. Watson got the change immediately.

After several years, Mr. Foster transferred his house and car to his wife's name. He put all his investments in trust funds for his children. Soon he even had his monthly salary automatically placed in his wife's checking account on the first of every month. Shortly after he freed himself of fear through this positive action, his wife ran away, taking the children with her. Mr. Foster's fears now turned to complete joy. He took his wife to court with such vengeance that he forgot his own persecution. As for Watson, he had to start building a new illusion for his boss.

THE TRIUMPH OF TECHNOLOGY Those afflicted with the technology bug envision a world where trivial duties are taken over by machines. People are meant for more than mechanical drudgery. In a plastic wonderland people sit and philosophize about new worlds for scientific know-how to conquer. The energy problem will be solved, peace will reign, and organizations will flourish throughout the earth.

Such happy optimists are heirs of the work ethic. They believe that people are the master of nature and that nature was meant to be subdued and controlled for their benefit. These types are easy to work with because of their unshakable faith in the future. They are untouched by the temporary trivial incidents in their profession; when they get low, you can refer to the inevitable goal of industrial fulfillment to lift their spirits.

Don't try to engage these dreamers in detail work. You have to approach them with a grand plan. And keep in mind that their optimism is valuable to your organization. They are the yeast that leavens the inert dough of change. You do everyone a favor if you help to foster their illusion.

As you read newspapers and magazines, you can add to this list of working models. Rehearse a few gently with your subjects to see which ones work best. Then create an illusion that will earn you an Academy Award for best screenplay.

One word of caution. As you begin working on your manipulatee, you must not oversimplify the illusion-making process. The working models described above are adequate for beginnings, but they are hardly ever found in their pure state.

Even the most optimistic futurist can become afflicted on short notice with an Inquisition fixation. Remember that people change with events, and it is your job to watch for signs of change so that you can reshape your illusion as the need arises.

Twenty-Four-Hour Protection Against a Stink

Whatever illusion you create, you will want to build in a few reinforcements—sort of deodorant protection against the stinking truth. These reinforcements are what you would call ''supporting materials'' in a written report. Although few people read anything but your two-page summary and conclusion, you have to have bulk in between. You therefore outline a pattern of reality and reinforce it to give it substance: you smear it with a strong deodorant.

One of the most effective forms of deodorant protection is *verbal verification.* By cultivating the same illusion with your subject's secretary and spouse you can validate your illusion by making it come from two seemingly independent sources.

One executive said in all seriousness, ''I know that's true. I've heard it from three different people.'' That attitude made Henry Luce, owner of *Time* and *Life,* one of the major reality shapers of this century. He controlled two of the three reality sources for Americans, and the third was the hometown newspaper that got most of its editorial views from *Time* and *Life.*

Written verification is also valuable support for deceptionists. A report published in a house organ increases in significance because so many people read it. That is why public relations people often attain powerful organizational control. These illusion shapers are frequently master deceptionists.

Whether your deception is an illusion-changing project or a simple twist of point of view, the more varied the support, the stronger the case. Violet worked in an office as personal secretary for the head of the department. She also had to work for the 15 department members, who regarded her time as their own. For two years she tried to convince her boss that secretarial duties should be reassigned to protect her from the department members' demands. "They need free access to you," he said, putting her protests aside.

Violet decided to put together a multilevel illusion package to convince her boss of her difficult position. She began a propaganda campaign with the department members. She pointed out that they deserved to have their own secretary who would be available to them at all times. It wasn't right that they take her leftover time for their many needs.

Simultaneously, she began a subtle slowdown for her boss. When he asked her if something had been done, she replied that she had been working with one of the department members and had not had a chance to get to it. With all the goodwill in the world, trying frantically to manage everything, she tangled up several important phone calls.

Violet also spread the illusion upward, through a secretary in another section. Finally, one of the boss's superiors mentioned that secretaries in other sections had a much clearer division of duties than Violet did. Even though the boss was half aware of what Violet was up to, he succumbed to her plan. It was much easier than training a new personal secretary, and everything did point to the validity of her demands.

With several kinds of evidence supporting your deception, your world view will meet your subjects wherever they look. But be careful. Don't believe any of it yourself. Your strength lies in your knowledge that reality itself is an illusion, one that can be twisted to please those who do not have your immunity to its enticing possibilities.

Dream Shaking

Sometimes you have to fight a defensive game by preventing other manipulators from building a world view that leaves you out. As soon as you see a contradictory deception developing, you must destroy it with an aggressive illusion of your own.

Suppose you find that older, senior managers in your organization are spreading the illusion that experience is the major basis for advancement. For your protection, you shatter that view with an illusion of your own: ability declines with age. To support that view, you point out that mathematicians, for example, are usually worn out by the time they are 30. Quietly you collect examples of high-level incompetence and use them in your dream-shaking campaign.

You may even find it useful to initiate refresher courses for senior executives. These courses, usually taught by younger managers, reinforce the idea that the old have to learn from the young. Such techniques can do a lot to upset the view that wisdom comes with age and seniority.

In shaking up dreams, you must be sure that you do not antagonize the real power. By placing emphasis on natural ability rather than age or experience, you can give the powerful ones the idea that they have always been brilliant, independent of position and age. Playing to these cherished beliefs will set older. managers squabbling among themselves and create the illusion that the young Turks have the ideas, the know-how, and the community spirit lacking in the supergrades.

Youth versus age is only one of many conflicting world views in business situation. Once you spot a troublesome view, you must develop an illusion to counteract it. Then devote part of your daily activity to destroying the contradictory pattern while pushing your own illusion with quiet, consistent vigor.

Shortcut to Failure

One of the quickest routes to failure for the deceptionist is lying. The best deceptions depend not on lies, but on truths. Occasionally you may have to resort to a small lie to save time; but if you start telling too many lies, you will make upkeep on deception unnecessarily cumbersome. The best manipulators know that truth is better than falsehood for prolonged deception.

If sudden pressure requires a quick lie, tell it with candor. Most people get so much sincerity in their voices when they lie that it is easy to sift the lie out of their other trivial discourse. Look down and let the lie come out somewhat hesitantly, as if you were really thinking about what you were saying. Then try to get some support for it as soon as possible. Turn it into the truth, retroactively.

One executive, asked how much overtime his computer crew put in, wanted to maintain the illusion of needing more staff. He said they were working as much as 20 hours a week in addition to their regular shifts. When he got back to the office to find that none of them had put in any overtime, he initiated a bonus for past work that went through the payroll as overtime. He also urged his crew to undertake a project that got them up to 20 hours a week overtime before the next pay period.

Such an *emergency lie* needs scrupulous support. Casual liars are certain to blunder into numerous contradictions that earn them unsavory reputations. Manipulators who save lies for emergencies are much more likely to maintain a high credibility rating.

At times the most truthful person sees a hurdle that cannot be leaped with absolute truth. In such difficult situations the *anticipated lie* is useful. Here you make preparations before rather than after the fact. Suppose you know you are going to be asked if you completed a report before July 1. You hurry to complete it—it's now August—and then prepare supporting documents dated and filed to indicate that the report has been completed for months, though not circulated. By the time the question arises, everyone is convinced that the report was filed away in early June. Unless, as with Nixon's tax contributions, someone is out to get you for other reasons, the anticipated lie works well.

If people are out to get you, the ultimate defense is the *admitted error.* When you are caught in a lie or a fault, you either plead confusion or make a hasty avowal of wrongdoing and throw yourself on the mercy of the people involved. A strong confession at the right time can do you as much good as a competent deception or all the lies you've told.

When it becomes obvious you are going to be found out, make a public statement of the whole affair, pointing out the confusions and pressures that led to your mistake. If you have any skill as a deceptionist, you will come out with your image enhanced by your innocence and honesty.

Ringing True

As you have already begun to notice, deceptions ring true only as long as you remain free from them. You are strong because you know that what seems to be reality is an illusion. Still, in a paradoxical way, you have to give yourself to a deception while you are participating in it. Like a stage actor, you throw yourself into the part completely, but you never believe you *are* the character you are portraying. If you do, you are likely to forget your lines and spoil the illusion.

You must be the character you are playing in the deception, but you must believe in the falsity of all the patterns you create. In other words, since all is false, all is equally true. You truly want power; you are truly diligent, worthy, ethical; you truly believe in your job and your organization. But if power, diligence, ethics, job, and organization ceased to exist, your freedom from illusion would guarantee you a successful place in any new reality to emerge. With that attitude, your deceptions will ring true.

In a recent interview a successful manager was quoted as

saying it was fortunate that both he and his company "believed in the Brooks Brothers look." We are all infinitely adjustable. That flexibility is what has made us one of the surviving species. We are what the environment demands we be. The contented executive honestly thought that he was a believer in Brooks Brothers. If he had grown up in a different environment, he might have been an equally ardent believer in "shirtsleeve management."

We ring true in our organization if we relax and accept the illusion that dominates at the moment. Our troubles begin when we feel that the illusion is the real thing—that "Brooks Brothers forever" is our motto and anyone who challenges it with a J. C. Penney leisure suit is unworthy of our attention. The wearer of that leisure suit may turn out to be Mr. Truepenny, who gets control of our section. Then leisure suits become the only acceptable apparel for the proper proletariat illusion.

Without becoming cynical, we must realize that reality changes from day to day. While we wear our button-down collars with conviction, we should be ready to scrap them when short tabs begin to show. The only way to continue ringing true is to know that the ultimate truth has not yet been achieved.

Devious Dan the Deception Man

Dan joined his company directly out of college. Within five years he became head of his department and changed the direction of the company. His major manipulative tool was deception.

JONES: What has been your major contribution to this department during your five years here?

DAN: I've remolded it into my own image.

JONES: What do you mean by that?

DAN: When I came here I was an amorphous mass. I could have taken any shape that was necessary for my advancement. I examined the department and found that most of the executives were over 40. The chance of getting any influence for the next 20 years was slight. Being optimistic, I decided that if I took the shape of the executives running the department I would be at the bottom for most of my career. The only thing to do was to make myself as different from them as possible.

JONES: What was their orientation?

DAN: They had developed a community attitude toward the department. It was service-directed, project-oriented. They turned out a lot of work with efficiency and cooperation. I knew that I was up against a winning combination.

JONES: Then how did you get to your present position so quickly?

DAN: I began to circulate the idea that research was superior to service. Gradually the executives began to feel defensive about their goals. They began to believe that the national trend was toward pure research, for which they were not suited. I played to their insecurity and fear.

They developed inferiority complexes and began to compete with me on my level. I conned some of them into believing they were wasting their time with the practical; they were too good to be working at the grimy stuff. Together we hired new people who had the same progressive attitude. As soon as the new people came in, we dropped the old-timers, who couldn't compete with our new jargon. They began to feel like has-beens.

JONES: Did you believe that research was superior to service?

DAN: Of course.

JONES: Under other circumstances would you have felt different about it?

DAN: What you want me to say is that I played to win. You're damn right I did. Everybody does. I won't say that the department is any better now than it was before. But it's doing what I want it to do: providing me with a good living and a way to the top. I'm still playing the research angle, but I can see that as conditions change I may have to shift to the service route to maintain control.

JONES: Can you recall any one moment when you knew you were going to be successful in restructuring your department's view? Was there a time when you were sure you had won?

DAN: I remember that one of the best moments—maybe the first one—was at a briefing session. The phrases I had been using were coming back to me out of the mouths of the oldsters. They were seeing the world that I had made for them and using the language of that world. I knew then that everything was going to work out my way.

JONES: Has anybody tried to use the same kind of deception on you?

DAN: Sure. Some of the old-timers tried, and one of the new people threw in with the old ones, but I'm flexible enough to bend under their efforts to climb up. I'm going to be around a long time. Anyway, you've got to keep moving: when you leave old illusions behind, you should have new ones ready up ahead. I don't think much about the past. I'm working on a new illusion now.

6

SLANDER

Screwing Up Reputations

SLANDER is a special variety of deception. Instead of developing a deceptive world view, you create a false picture of an individual. The picture is designed to dehumanize people so that they become one-dimensional caricatures, dominated by a single unattractive feature that obscures all their redeeming qualities.

As we saw in the last chapter, everyone likes to oversimplify. It is much easier to mark people as dullards, fools, or geniuses than to continue responding to them as complex human beings. Since the tendency to pigeonhole people is so common, slander should be handled carefully. Like an electrician with a live wire, you must have deep respect for its destructive power.

Every generalization you make about someone contributes to a composite picture. Attitude has a lot to do with whether these generalizations constitute slander. Malicious tales designed to sully someone's reputation may be slanderous even if they are partially true. Idle gossip about someone's nasty personality may also cause wanton destruction.

The trouble with dirtying another person's reputation is that the act quickly gets out of hand. Conditions around the two of you may change so fast that you end up as the screwee. You slander a person as a "crazy theorist." Two years later, when people are tired of drudgery, the term is translated into "delightful eccentric." Your subject wins the favor you've been trying to take from him.

To be successful, slander must be premeditated. Thoughtless backstabbing will simply earn you the reputation of a badmouther. You slander only when the act accomplishes an otherwise unachievable but necessary purpose. Many people, frustrated and disappointed with their own existence, become chronic slanderers. Their conversation is largely a running commentary on how vile everyone is. Overslandering, like overeating, destroys the pleasure and the purpose of the act.

Judicious slander comes out of a positive, constructive attitude toward the world. If you malign others continually, perceptive listeners soon suspect that you slander them when they are not around. Generally, you should undertake only one active slander campaign at a time. Anything more than that marks you as a malcontent or troublemaker.

At the beginning of your campaign make sure that you cover the purpose of your slander with great care. If it is obvious that you are going to gain personally because of what you say, your slander will immediately become suspect. If you have previously been on bad terms with your intended victim, you have to restore good feelings before you begin your campaign. Goodwill toward a victim is the first step in a professional screw job. Flowers of evil do not grow in unprepared soil. You must set the peat moss and fertilizer around the roots of the rose you are encouraging to bloom.

When your preparations are complete, find an appropriate image to place on your subject, just as you found the right illusion in shaping your deceptions. Every personality suggests its opposite, its shadow image. It is easy to call attention to the vile shadow rather than the shining self. If your subject is known for a jolly, outgoing nature, twist that image to one of a smiling hypocrite. If your victim is by nature shy and retiring, peg him as superior and standoffish, hard to get to know. These

shadow images pave the way for a successful slander campaign. Like deception, slander works best when it is based on
the truth. You build better on solid ground than on shifting
sand. Find the true center of your subject's personality and
then build an undesirable, shadow image around it.

Preparing the Image

Four executives who ate together every day spent a week
contriving a special slander project. On Monday one of them
asked, ''If you really wanted to hurt somebody in this organization, what is the worst image you could put on him?'' Each
day one of them presented a favorite image and explained why
it would be the worst to lay on another manager. At the end of
the week they voted on the worst slander possible in their
organization. They passed up ''dishonest,'' ''shiftless,'' and
''dull'' and voted unanimously for ''troublemaker.''

These executives were engaged in preslanderous investigation. They were checking local attitudes to see what images
were particularly abhorrent that year. With the information
they derived from their luncheons they went back to their
departments prepared to slander someone more efficiently
than ever before.

In most offices slanderous terms circulate freely. Shrewd
slanderers make sure their terms circulate more frequently
than the others. They work unobtrusively, maintaining a pleasant relationship with their victims while quietly suggesting to
others, ''I don't know Arnie very well but . . .'' or ''Everybody who knows Sarah says . . .'' Such simple remarks
permanently brand people with images of the slanderer's
choice.

Like all good manipulators, successful slanderers avoid
emotional involvement. They know that cool objectivity is essential to their campaign. Donna's attempt is an example of
how a slander campaign should *not* be conducted.

Donna found she was being pushed aside by a younger manager. She was left with the busywork while Sue got the inter-

esting jobs. Deeply angered by the new situation, she noticed that Sue and the director occasionally went out for lunch together. The next time they left together, Donna decided to use sexual slander to destroy Sue. She went around asking others in her department, ''Have you noticed how close Sue and the boss are? I wonder if his wife knows yet.''

Her anger at her own situation caused her to push the supposed affair wherever she went. Soon everyone assumed—as people are likely to do if someone is truly bent on slander— that Sue and the director were sleeping together during lunch hour. The department divided into those who felt it was disgusting to mix business with pleasure and those who thought nothing was wrong with some harmless fun. It never occurred to anyone to wonder if it was actually happening.

Even the director's superiors, who had called the original luncheon meetings he and Sue had attended, began to talk about the director's unbusinesslike behavior. The director's wife grew angry and alienated. And the more the director denied it, the more people smiled at his guilty squirming.

But for her trouble Donna, the instigator of the slander, achieved nothing. She was more wretched than before because she wondered if there really was something between Sue and the director. She had always secretly admired him and wanted him for herself. She had created the slander not out of a necessary purpose, but out of selfish hatred and desire. Her slander led to further unhappiness and resentment and deterioration of her work. After several years Donna took a more boring job to get away from her misery.

Such undirected image building has no value. Only coolly dispassionate slandering can succeed. If you are emotionally involved with your victim, get it over with before you begin your manipulation. Love and hatred have no place in a slander campaign. Unemotional realists control the public world.

As we saw earlier in this chapter, the choice of an appropriate image is an essential first step in slandering. Although theoretically you can impose almost any kind of image on someone, it is best to select an existing trait and ascribe vile motives to it. Milt found it necessary to knife Andy. He began by unobtrusively observing Andy's daily work habits. Andy had a great many consulting projects and was often out of town. Although these trips were endorsed and even encouraged by the boss, Milt decided that the most reasonable slander was that of "department ghost."

The next time Andy was away on a business trip, Milt said to a friend at coffee, "Isn't it convenient to have two places you're supposed to be? That way if anybody asks, you can always have your secretary say you're in the other one—like Andy."

When Andy was away on another business trip, Milt took a dustcloth and marched through several offices saying that he was on his way to clean off Andy's desk. So much dust had accumulated that it was activating Milt's allergy. Still another time, Milt took up a collection for "The Deceased, Andy."

The slander was committed with such good humor—and sometimes directly to Andy's face—that no one took Milt seriously until he had achieved his purpose. After Milt had ceased openly joking about Andy's absence, others began remarking on it. "Isn't Andy clever to get so much work done by his secretary? He's never here to do it."

The first time a slipup occurred in Andy's department, the boss assumed it was because Andy had not been around to supervise. When he talked to Andy about it, Andy got mad: "If you don't want me to leave my desk, I don't see how you can expect me to do consultations."

The upshot was that Milt soon got control of the areas Andy had previously managed. Nobody noticed Milt's shortcomings. They were too busy describing Andy's. Milt had wisely prepared an image that was now an inseparable part of Andy's job—and that image destroyed him.

Slander is a constant in every organization. If you are not actively aware of it, you are likely to be the victim of it. Later in this chapter you will find out how to become screwproof.

For now, keep in mind that you cannot protect yourself unless you know how to use the techniques of slander offensively as well as defensively.

Screwing It In

Slanderers depend on repetition to give their images the semblance of truth. If you circulate enough copies of the same false image, you will soon obscure the real one. Knowing the value of reiteration, careful slanderers develop *image clusters*, groups of related words that reinforce a particular idea. A slanderer who wants to give someone the image of a superficial thinker will use such words as "clown," "showoff," "fool," "courtjester," "triviamaster," "playboy." At every opportunity the slanderer helps the campaign along. A friend at the next desk is turning through the daily paper and puts the comic sheet aside. The slanderer laughs and says, "That reminds me of our office comic." By frequent repetition of phrases and stories, the slanderer imposes the central image permanently on a subject.

The creative use of image clusters is the hallmark of a successful smear campaign. A talented slanderer is a poet shaping a single image out of a mass of verbal symbols. The slander becomes a work of art that satisfies people's esthetic sense.

These clusters don't have to be elaborate. The best slandering is done with a minimum of effort. When Milt did such a thorough job on Andy, he spent most of his time watching the image he had placed on Andy get screwed into place by subsequent events. If you select images wisely, time will do the rest.

In any organization certain events happen regularly; people respond to these recurrent situations the same way every time. Armed with these two pieces of information, you lay out your three-step slander campaign: (1) you watch your slander victim during several of these recurrent situations; (2) you prepare your image clusters to highlight the victim's unattractive response to the situation; and (3) whenever the situation happens next, you screw him to the wall with the clusters you have prepared beforehand.

Here are some typical situations and responses, along with suggested image clusters. You will want to add your own ones to the list.

Deadlines. People are always tense as deadlines approach, but they respond to these occasions in different ways. Controlled personalities who have planned ahead seem to be calm, but any hint that they have forgotten something sends them into a tailspin. To slander them, you build images that play on their controlled nature. They are cold, unfeeling automatons. They are aloof, uninvolved, and dense. When they get flustered they can't take the pressure: they become untied, distracted, addled scarecrows in a high wind.

High-strung types reveal their tenseness at deadline time by growing irritable. Here you point out their selfishness, their irrationality and emotionalism, their inability to control their feelings. Without making any effort to change their behavior, you increase their tension and wrath by making others sensitive to it.

Easygoing types calmly and willingly submit to working overtime to meet deadlines. You peg them as fall guys, patsies, people who try to make everyone else in the office look bad by taking on extra duties. Everybody hates bootlickers.

Errors discovered. Whenever an error has been discovered, some people feel guilty immediately; others assume it is not their fault; still others look for someone else to blame it on. Whatever kind your victim is, you can spot the type and have your images ready the next time an error occurs.

With the guilt-ridden, by far the most numerous variety, you do not attribute guilt but simply call attention to its manifestations: "Look at old redface. His hands must be dirty—he won't even.take them out of his pockets. Too bad everyone has to suffer for someone else's mistakes." In this situation, of course, your stance must be one of complete innocence. With all humility—after all, anybody can make a mistake—you make the guilt-ridden spirit feel even more ashamed.

With the blameless types, you have to work a little harder to get an image screwed on. They feel no guilt and are likely to stay in the background; most people passively resent them. They are "high and mighty," "too good to be true," "notoriously insensitive." Their aloofness makes you wonder if they care about their professional responsibilities. They are "lying mighty low," like "a rabbit in a cabbage patch" or a "fox near a chickenhouse."

Scapegoating types are the most verbal and the easiest to nail. When they respond actively to the discovered error, you can designate them as the office troublemakers. Everything would have been all right if they had just kept their mouths shut. Some people will do anything to get ahead. They've always had it in for the guilty party, and now they can't wait to knife him. It's indecent and inhuman. Nobody but a beast would be so quick to take unfair advantage.

Promotion time. Tempers and feelings are at their rawest at promotion time, when money and position are at stake. This is a perfect time to drag out your image-fixing kit and get to work. On money matters, personalities typically divide into three types: aggressive, passive-receptive, and desperate. With each of these types you get your image clusters ready and, when promotion time comes along, trot them out.

For the aggressive types, you can call attention to their greedy, self-seeking opportunism. You suppose push has taken the place of ability in their thinking, but you hope the organization still has some respect for good taste and responsibility. If, on the other hand, you are working with a passive personality, you can easily point out that inertia and mediocrity are fine for lower positions, even desirable, but leadership positions require an energy that expresses itself in vigorous, positive action.

Perhaps the easiest type to handle at promotion time is the desperate person who falls to pieces under the pressure. The image to impose here is one of emotional instability. A single stain will spread all over the desperate one's reputation if you simply point out signs of emotional weakness as they appear— sweaty palms, shifty eyes, trembling hands, anything that denotes lack of control.

These are only samples of the kind of creative power you can unleash once you get in the habit of watching for tension points in your office. When tensions rise, be ready to go modestly to work. The image you create for them will stick for years, because it is not so much an image as an inner truth about the victim's personality that is finally brought to the surface.

Another Twist of the Screw

In addition to consciously planting image clusters, clever slanderers use trivial, undirected gossip to sow seeds that will grow into the images of their choice. Most people who are not talking about themselves are talking about other people. At dinner, cocktails, or golf, somebody asks, "Have you heard about John's weekend?" Then everyone's off with harmless gossip.

The difference between gossip and slander is that the latter is malicious, persistent, and purposeful. That purpose is the slanderer's strength. Shrewd slanderers hide their purpose under the guise of aimless comments. The discovery of image patterns is made by the listener, not the slanderer.

Most executive activities are so specialized that they are difficult subjects for casual conversation. The old "How's business?" that drew a long economic discourse two generations ago is no longer appropriate. People spend their lives with detailed reports and conferences that even they have no interest in. Now we are thrown back on personalities for our discussions.

Executives who spend much of their time analyzing and evaluating transfer this process to informal discussion. "Ron was off his game last weekend. Seemed tense. Wonder if he's having trouble at home?" Thus it begins—the motive-seeking evaluation of another personality. The gossip asks casual questions, attributing meaning without proof. Into this desultory conversation the slanderer intrudes a carefully prepared generalization. "Guess Ron can't be trusted any longer. He's always been something of an elitist."

The gossips latch on to this conclusion and store it away for future use, with some comment such as "Oh, I've been wondering what kind of guy he is." The slanderer caters to people's need for such oversimplification, offering a single tag word that sums up the victim's complex personality. After that, the gossips have a clearer focus for their stories. And the slanderer scores again.

Screw Proofing

Slander, like the atom bomb, should be reserved for emergencies. But it is used so often by inexperienced manipulators that you need to develop some fairly powerful tactics against it. At its best, defense against slander absorbs a great deal of your energy and thought. At its worst, it separates you from people who share your values and interests—interests that, pursued in honesty, would lead to more efficient management. Slanderers make sure that no one can accomplish anything except in a miasma of suspicion and distrust.

Ignore slanderers and others see you with the stained image they have created. Fight them head on and you are accused of antagonistic behavior, marked as difficult to work with, and smeared in every encounter with your detractors. Clever slanderers can shape an unpleasant image around you no matter what response you offer.

Without becoming paranoid, you have to accept the possibility that in the course of your career somebody will try to get a knife between your shoulder blades. You will have to learn to watch for the danger signals without expending unnecessary energy doing so.

You may go for months or years without any active antagonism; then for some reason, usually professional jealousy or increased competition, someone will start a slander campaign against you. The sooner you are aware of it, the sooner you can start your defense. Be on the alert whenever a change occurs in your organization. A new person comes in at your level or higher, authority is reshuffled in some way, somebody retires. When change accelerates, tension increases; and slander thrives on tension.

You may notice that your colleagues are more tense than usual and seem to have a different attitude toward you. Instead of being easy and relaxed, they are slightly guarded, reserved, almost watchful. Occasionally you may catch covert glances that make you wonder if your nose is dirty. Maybe you are getting a bad cold or the flu.

If you don't start sneezing in a day or two, it could be a slanderer instead of a virus. You have no idea who it is, but somebody's working on you. You play into his hands at this point if you begin to change your relationships with others or grow surly and obnoxious. Then he could point out how guilty you have been acting lately, and your response would validate his slander.

Insofar as possible, then, continue the same general attitudes and relationships you have always maintained. Don't become upset or alienated. If the slanderer can cut you off from others, he can project whatever image he wants on you. No one will be listening to your protests.

While you continue running a smooth course, keep a careful eye out for someone who is more friendly than usual. Among the cooling, suspicious relationships you will note one warm spot. Someone is smiling more than usual. If he is an experienced slanderer he will try to disguise his increased warmth, but he has to maintain some friendliness toward you so that others think he is well meaning. That warm spot in the cold universe is the source of your slanderous image.

When you have made sure you have a good suspect, start your defensive action.

Unscrewing

The best defense against slanderers is an understanding of the various images they manipulate. We have already seen how slanderers build image clusters for their victims. Now let's take a closer look at the specific images involved.

The first image to be concerned with is your *self-image,* the way you think of yourself most of the time. If you are not honest with yourself about your strengths and weaknesses, about where you grew up, who your parents are, what your major goals are, you are going to be easy prey for slanderers. If they can cause your self-image to totter, you are doomed. Unless your self-image is founded on firm reality, slanderers can make you seem and feel phony and insincere. They can shake your self-confidence so that you are unable to maintain honest, open relationships with your associates.

Clyde, for example, had always tried to hide his ghetto origins. He was ashamed of the poverty he and his parents had endured. When he was with people from more affluent backgrounds, his unresolved self-image made him unpredictable—sometimes shy, sometimes excessively aggressive. A slanderer, seeing this inconsistency, began to imply that Clyde was secretive because of dishonesty. The result was a noticeable loss of credibility for Clyde.

In contrast to your self-image is your *projected image,* the way others see you. Although you may see yourself as a shy, decent person, others may interpret your shyness as sullenness, sulkiness, or some other undesirable characteristic.

To find out what your projected image is, you should talk honestly with your associates about the way you appear at work. You have to be open and willing to accept the truth about how you project. Ask carefully selected people to tell you frankly what you're like, what others are saying about you. Wise managers rely on several trusted sources for feedback about their projected image.

When Ernie came to his new job, he didn't know that he was being set up by a slanderer, but Hank was working on him. Hank took a look at Ernie's advanced degree from Cal Tech and immediately decided that Ernie was proud of his education. When he discovered that Ernie had an undergraduate degree from the University of Wyoming, Hank was sure that Ernie had a lot of pride in his academic achievement. That pride was the way to successful slander for Hank. Ernie had not been on the job a week before Hank was suggesting that Ernie felt superior to everyone else.

It was partly true. Ernie was young and tended to sneer at ignorance because he had fought against it so long in his struggle for an education. His quiet competence was read as snobbishness. In the first year, thanks to Hank's introductory slander, Ernie was lonely, wretched in his position. He had no friends at work and was beginning to wonder if he should look around for another job.

Then one of his superiors called him in. "I wonder if you realize how you offend people by sneering at them," he said to Ernie.

Ernie turned red at the man's directness and at his own guilt. "I don't mean to."

"I'm not telling you how to act," the boss said, "but I think you should know how easily offended people can be by demonstrations of educational superiority. It can make working together difficult."

Ernie thanked the man and went back to his desk to think about it. He had probably been a pretty insensitive, callow youth. Ernie decided to work on changing his projected image. It wasn't easy, but it was the beginning of a counter campaign that destroyed Hank's slander and made Ernie's working relationships infinitely more pleasant.

Ernie was lucky that one person came forward to talk honestly with him about his projected image. If you are a slander victim, you may have to seek out sources—from superiors, subordinates, or equals—to get an unbiased appraisal of how you project to others. Even if you discover that there is some foundation to the slander, don't let the realization spoil your sense of self-worth. Maintain your ability to readjust to human relationships and you can usually correct any damage the slanderer may have caused.

Ted, who prided himself on his emotional warmth, was judged by his associates as cold and distant. In his efforts to control his naturally affectionate, outgoing personality, he had overcompensated and projected an aloofness that offended some of the people who worked with him. A slanderer, seeing the difference between Ted's self-image and his projected one, played on the contrast. Unfortunately, no one told Ted what was happening. He became more and more remote, much to his own harm.

Only by being in control of your self-image and your projected image can you protect yourself against an imposed image, the one the slanderer is trying to put on you. The slanderer, who has constructed the imposed image out of your projected one, is dependent for success on a continued projection of that general image. A change in your public image can destroy the slanderer's work. Here is how to defend yourself against an imposed image.

Suppose you have reason to believe someone is out to malign you. Your best defense is to launch an image-changing offensive. If you have been absorbed in your work and have neglected human relationships, spend more time cultivating people. If you have been cultivating people and neglecting your work, spend a little more time at your desk.

Don't make the change suddenly and visibly; shift your emphasis subtly so that you gradually project a new image. Don't get ruffled if you have to spend time and effort changing your projected image. Accept it as part of the job.

The new image you projected is likely to thwart the slanderer, who has been busily building on the old one. He will look ludicrous if he says that you are goofing off while you turn in a huge report you have been working on for six months. He is going to feel like a fool—and look like one—if he says you pay no attention to human relationships while you are having a dinner party for half the office staff next Saturday night.

If you keep your public image flexible, you will always be one step ahead of your detractors. In a fast stream you have to paddle faster than the current to gain control of your boat's direction. In a slander defense you move faster than the slanderer to gain control of the image he is trying to impose on you.

If you suspect that you are being slandered, launch a small

counterattack. Don't plan a brutal retaliation or confrontation; imply pityingly that the person must have a deep-seated, irrational resentment toward you to resort to such lowdown tricks. Innocently ask associates from time to time why the slanderer always baits you. Don't come on strong, but smile and ridicule the whole effort.

If you are wrong, and no slander has been circulating, your gentle offensive stance will not hurt anyone, because you are not making direct accusations. If the slander has been spread, your casual attitude toward it will project a good image and ease any tensions among your associates.

The goal of your counterattack is not to slander the slanderer, but to reveal the obvious falsity of the image he has tried to impose. In the process, of course, you will reveal him as the evil wisher he is. Emasculate the villain and you probably won't get screwed by him again.

Surviving is worth the effort. And you will survive if you keep cool while the slanderer hangs himself on the reality of your firmly projected, but constantly shifting public image. Remember, though, that the game is over when you have won. Resentment and continued antagonism are not worth the tension they produce. Watch the former slanderer for the poisonous snake he is, but don't let anger or lingering hatred sap your strength or sully your projected image.

Ivan and Ruth the Slander Victims

Slander victims are somewhat shy about discussing their retaliative techniques, but most executives have a slander story. Here are two of them.

JONES: Have you ever been the victim of slander?

IVAN: I don't know that I'd call it that. That makes it sound so portentous. I've had plenty of people try to stab me in the back.

JONES: Were they successful?

IVAN: Sometimes they won; sometimes I did. I remember the best one, though. He ended up helping me along.

JONES: How was that?

IVAN: Seven of us met every Monday morning with the director to discuss budget and policy. One of the department
heads was a sneaking schemer. I knew that, and he made
me mad, so I would sulk and growl at him. He was the
friendly kind—always a smile and a handshake. I hated
the bastard.

    After about a year the director called me in and told
me I was making cooperation difficult because of my antagonistic personality. I realized then that the bastard had
been playing me for the villain, and the other department
heads had accepted me in that role. Since I had no other
regular meetings with them, the only time they saw me—
Monday mornings—I was surly. They had been developing programs with the other guy and leaving me out.

JONES: So what did you do?

IVAN: I thanked the director for the honest talk, and went
back to work. At the next meeting, I didn't sit in my
regular chair. I opened the draperies and sat down with
my back to the window, opposite the slanderer, so that
when he looked at me he had to gaze into the sun. Naturally, every time he looked at me he frowned. I began
talking, laughing, joking. After the meeting I mentioned to
one of the department heads that the slanderer must have
had a bad weekend from the frowns he was giving me.

    After two or three weeks the roles were reversed. My
drastic personality shift had thrown my opponent off balance. He grew quiet and confused as I became more ani-
mated toward the others.

    When the director had to be out of town for several
weeks, he chose me to chair the group. My old slanderer
had to be my friend because it was obvious I was in the
favored spot. He's taken his slander somewhere else now.

    The second slander victim was not so successful in her de-
fense. Here's Ruth's story.

JONES: Have you had any trouble with slanderers?

RUTH: I certainly have. One of them ruined me, and I didn't even know it till it was too late to do anything.

JONES: How did it happen?

RUTH: A new woman came into our department, innocent, inexperienced, and anxious. She took me to lunch and let me play the guide role. I enjoyed talking to her because she reminded me of what I had been when I started working there. I told her what I thought of everybody in the department—which ones to watch out for, which ones to count on.

After a few weeks she dropped me. I didn't think much about it except to assume she was getting involved in her own circle. Within a month, though, I noticed that some of my relationships were changing. People didn't talk to me the way they used to. When I saw the new woman replacing me in the coffee room, I started snarling at her whenever I had a chance. Pretty soon I didn't have a friend in the place.

When I was told the company was restructuring and had to let me go, I asked the personnel manager what the real reason was. "You're a disruptive personality," he said. "Your work is all right, but your personal relationships have made you undesirable. We've got statements from most of the people in your department."

I got a job in another agency and tried to be positive, but it was difficult. I looked again for the worst in people. One day I ran into a guy from the old agency. He got to talking and the whole story came out. The new woman that I had talked personalities with had quoted me to the others. She had emphasized my negative comments and marked me as the malcontent. I ended up playing the role she had designed for me from the beginning: the fall guy.

JONES: Did you ever do anything about it?

RUTH: No. I've settled down in my new job. That was another world. I messed it up, but I'm glad I found out what happened. From now on, I'm going to be me, not what somebody else says I am.

7

THREAT

Finding the Fear

THE HUMAN condition is so uncertain that no one is completely immune to fear. Good manipulators find their subjects' secret fears and play on them with threats to their security. These threats arouse fear and discomfort and provide manipulators with the opportunity to control the choices and actions of their victims.

Threats can be intended or unintended. *Intended threats* are those the manipulator consciously develops to control the manipulatee. When Jack repeatedly interrupted Jane while she was trying to make a report at a staff meeting, she looked him in the eye and, with cool humor, said, "If you interrupt me one more time, I'm going to throw this water jug at you." With the right jesting tone Jane made her point without her pitch.

The intended threat is most effective when it is carefully chosen and fitted to the occasion. Even though Jane and Jack were enemies, Jane's cool delivery kept the tension down. It would have been a mistake for Jane to let her built-up resentment explode into some hysterical scene. All she wanted at the moment was the attention of her audience. Her controlled response was the key to her success. Jane used the threat to accomplish a specific purpose—increased effectiveness in presenting her report—not to vent her anger on an old opponent.

Let's look at an occasion when an intended threat can be simple but serious. After he had submitted an article to a scientific journal, Ben found out that an old enemy from his graduate school days was editing the journal and had decided to review the article himself. Since the journal was the most prestigious in the field, Ben was not willing to withdraw his submission and send it somewhere else. What could he do to make sure that his article was accepted?

Searching for an appropriate threat, Ben reviewed the editor's past. Any unethical or shameful behavior from graduate school would have been extremely useful. An allusion to it in his next letter might have frightened the editor into publishing Ben's article. Unfortunately, Ben could remember nothing worth developing into an intended threat.

He then investigated the editor's present situation. He knew no one on the journal's editorial board or its board of trustees. Ben read back issues of the journal in the hope of finding some gross error in editorial policy that he could threaten to reveal. But the man's editorial job seemed impeccable.

Then Ben began to think of ambitions the editor might be entertaining. If Ben could threaten to slow the man's professional growth in some way, he would have an intended threat worth implementing. In talking to people around the country about the editor, he learned that the man had applied for a National Science Foundation grant for the next year. Ben's old roommate from college was now on the review board for NSF applications. He had found his intended threat.

Ben corrected a few footnotes in a Xerox copy of his article and sent it to the editor, along with a friendly note asking the editor to make the changes. In a short postscript, Ben added, "I hear from my old friend Sam Steuben, who is now on the grants board, that you are applying for an NSF grant. I certainly wish you luck with that application." In the veiled language of the intended threat, this postscript was all Ben needed to get his article lead position in the next issue of the journal.

If Ben's article had been hopelessly bad, the editor would have had to decide whether the threat of publishing a bad article outweighed the threat of losing an NSF grant. As it was, the article was pretty good. Ben achieved only what he deserved from the beginning: an honest reading. In the give-and-take of professional life, threats are often used to counteract old antagonisms that play an unjust but decisive role in business decisions.

Ben never actually talked to his friend on the NSF board. It is quite likely that his friend would not have been influenced by Ben's word about the editor, and that other members of the panel would not have followed Ben's friend's recommendation. But the editor had to weigh those chances against the chance of losing a grant that he wanted. Here the intended threat got Ben what he wanted and cost the editor nothing.

At times you will have to develop an intended threat over a long period of time, sustaining it with thought and effort. The techniques you learn in this chapter will help you construct more complex threat systems.

Unintended threats are ones generated by the situation itself. They may exist before anyone is aware of them. One of your colleagues does not know how to make small talk, has no facility for human exchange, is self-conscious except when he is at the drafting board. If you treat him the same way you treat everybody else—relaxed and easy—your awkward colleague will begin quietly maligning you. People will start avoiding you, and your relationships at work will become tense and strained. Unless you neutralize the unintended threat, Mr. Awkward will do all he can to make you as wretched and insecure as you are making him feel.

For some maladjusted and wretched people, the presence of certain co-workers is a gross offense. In one office such a pitiful creature came to work one day with a pistol and shot two fellow managers. The wounded executives said they knew of no reason for the attack. They should have known that their crime was living in the presence of the maladjusted person.

The psychiatrist who examined the attacker discovered that the man had felt threatened for several years by these two successful associates and had alleviated his tension the only way he knew how—by destroying those causing the tension.

The trouble with unintended threats is that they must be anticipated in order to be controlled. Once they are recognized, they can be transferred from the unintended area to the intended area and then used with discretion.

The example of the psychotic pistol carrier indicates the main breeding ground for unintended threats: personal differences. In a culture as diverse as ours, where people from many regions and social levels work side by side, such differences are bound to arise. Only a keen eye to class, regional, or ethnic dissimilarities can free us from the potential dangers of unintentional threats—whether we are the threatener or the victim.

Expected response is the place to look for unintended threats. Suppose you terminate a conversation with your usual parting phrase: "So long, see you later." If your listener walks off without saying anything, you may feel threatened by the "unnaturalness" of this response. On the other hand, your listener may be accustomed to saying nothing at the end of a conversation and may find your traditional parting phony and slightly threatening.

Both patterns are widespread in American business. Until you recognize them for what they are—superficial regional differences—they may turn into unintended threats. People are conditioned to expect certain responses from others. To avoid being a threat to them, you have to remain as neutral as possible until you become aware of areas where differences are likely to take on a threatening tone: at meetings, at lunch, at the water fountain, at places where money is being handled or finances discussed.

At such times you must watch for subtle signs of tension—slight changes in facial expressions or physical gestures. Then analyze the situation to see if differences in expected response are interfering with smooth communication and creating an unintended threat. When you know what these differences are, you can transfer them to your intended list and use them when necessary to your own advantage.

Later in this chapter you will find more examples of intended and unintended threats. Each example should alert you to other possible trouble spots. Until you are skillful in recognizing potential threats, you will be vulnerable to others and less than successful in controlling your own threat manipulation.

Overstepping

Konrad Lorenz's book *On Aggression* demonstrates the importance of natural territories. Certain physical areas cannot be invaded without seriously disturbing the aggressor-owner relationship. Manipulators can apply these observations to their office habitat. At times you will want to threaten territorial invasion to arouse the protective instincts of your subjects. At other times you will want to enter their territory quietly. Occasionally you will want to avoid their territory altogether.

Here's a common example of territorial intrusion. You notice that whenever you go to the supply cabinet for stationery, the secretary becomes sullen and uncooperative for several days. You ask what's wrong, and she says, "Oh, nothing." She really means it; she doesn't know what's wrong. But you begin to notice that other people ask her for their supplies. The supply cabinet, though she is unaware of it, is her territory. Crossing the boundary in front of the cabinet door is an infringement on her preserve.

Next time you need paper, you ask her for some. She grumbles that you are interrupting her work—people are always bugging her—but she loves it. The right to grumble is part of the love-play ritual that goes with getting stationery.

Many cherished physical territories around the office can become tension points. Using someone's phone without making the correct entry noises can disrupt a friendship. Going into someone's desk to find a stamp can be a heinous crime. Even though most people keep only junk in their desk, they regard it as an extension of their bodies. Opening their desk is the equivalent of unzipping their fly. Unless you have special permission to be there, you'd better leave it closed.

Restricting and expanding territories is one way of manipulating through threat. Grady was an incompetent, slovenly manager who rarely did the minimum amount assigned him, but he had been around so long that no one knew what to do about it. A new manager took over and decided to force Grady out with threats to Grady's territory. He gave Grady's few remaining duties to other people. Grady never missed them. He spent more time than ever chatting with his secretary.

Then one day Grady came to work to find that his secretary had been assigned to someone else. Grady, seeing a threat, went to the manager, who mumbled something about budget cuts. Grady returned to his desk and spent the rest of the day gossiping with friends on the phone. The manager had the phone taken out and moved Grady into an office with three other people. Grady was still not seriously aware of the threat pattern.

Finally, the manager touched Grady's essential territory. He asked Grady to share a desk. Grady resigned because, as he said, "no self-respecting manager can survive without a place to call his own."

You can usually tell when you are about to tread on private property. When you ask to use a telephone and the owner hesitates ever so slightly, say, "Oh, that's all right. I'll go to the outer office." Any cringing, hesitating, blinking, or tensing of fingers or shoulders should warn you to step back. Sometimes the threatened owner will shift backward or glance from side to side like a cornered animal. These danger signals suggest that you are intruding on territory where you don't belong. Unless intrusion is part of your threat manipulation, move back with a smile. Even your withdrawal must seem unobtrusive, since guilt and personal shame may be aroused if your subjects realize their irrationality.

When your success depends on establishing dominance, move forcefully into occupied territory with a display of power strong enough to quell any resistance. Moreover, when you have to commit an act of aggression, make sure you follow through. Don't launch an offensive and then fall back. That's worse than not starting one at all.

To become dominant, you must stalk your prey with slow, sure purpose. Weaker people will cringe as you sit on the edge of their desk. They won't like it, but you are establishing necessary dominance. You can encroach further on their personal sphere by putting your hand on their shoulder, pushing closer than they like, or indicating your control in other physical ways. They will usually relinquish their territory and submit to manipulation.

Once you have established your dominance, your victims will react like sullen children, crying out for further abuse. After you have sat with your foot propped on the edge of their desk, your hand resting carelessly on their telephone, they will accept your control with relief. You have taken over their guidance, they are free of that responsibility as long as you are around.

When such action is necessary for your purpose, perform it firmly. Never, though, use physical aggression to gratify your own power needs. If you assert territoriality aimlessly, you will lose control. The resentment and hatred you breed accomplish nothing. A conquering hero is everyone's favorite; a petty tyrant is nobody's friend.

When the territory is not physical but psychological, follow the same process. You ask about someone's family, health, income, age, rank, or seniority. Then watch to see which questions tread on private psychological ground. Unless your purpose demands passage, move back.

You can challenge psychological territories with either written or oral threats. *Verbal invasion* is simple and effective.

When someone starts a sentence, you finish it. The sentence is his territory. Since it is his creation, he feels the affection for it that expectant parents feel for their child. To cut it off before full term is painful. Invade enough and you shut your victim up altogether—or at least control his verbal reproductive system.

You don't always have to interrupt directly. At a meeting, for example, when someone is trying to make a telling point, you can whisper, cough, or move around the room. Any distraction is a threat to the person's territory and a gesture of invasion.

The ordinary rules of genteel behavior do not apply in territorial invasion. Aggressive people can control committee meetings by speaking up without waiting to be recognized. Those whose manners restrict them from challenging the chair fail to enter the verbal feeding ground in time to share the feast. Verbal invasion must be suited to the occasion, not some abstract rule of politeness.

When verbal aggressiveness is not convenient, you can attack through the written word. Make sure you can find a flaw in your victim's argument—an easy task once you upset a subject emotionally—and then come through with a *written invasion* that calls attention to the fact that you are taking over. A short, cogent memo, with copies sent to appropriate superiors, stills the growls from those whose territory you are trampling.

Remember, you are out to win, not to destroy utterly. A written territorial invasion is generally more forceful and lasting than a verbal one. When you have made a quick oral intrusion, you can withdraw and repair the breach with a friendly exchange later on. A verbal intrusion at one committee meeting can be smoothed over by an apology at the next meeting. Such a public withdrawal from occupied territory is usually enough to restore peace.

The written word, though, is permanent; it can be read over and over. It is a constant reminder to the person whose private preserve has been breached. After your victim has read your insult a dozen times, you will be unable to eradicate the impression seared on his brain. If hatred and ill will are what you are after, the written invasion is the quickest and most effective way to achieve it.

In writing you are unable to study the immediate reaction to your invasion, as you can when you are speaking directly to someone. Consequently, you may be going too far without an opportunity to know how deeply you've penetrated. Usually, it is wise to use written territorial invasion only after direct verbal attempts have failed.

One of the most sensitive psychological territories is a person's past. To invade this area uninvited is to stir up all kinds of protective behavior. If you know what you are doing, you can gain control—either by showing respect for treasured memories or by grabbing them and using them to your advantage.

Assume you know a person is secretly ashamed of the school he graduated from. If you want to ingratiate yourself, you make it clear that although you are his educational superior it doesn't matter. You know some wonderful people who graduated from Beatitudes Institute. You find some slightly inferior school to mention, and soon you are both threat-free, sneering at someone else. If, on the other hand, you want to dominate, you wield the educational disadvantage like a whip. And it does not have to be an inferior school. With the right aggressive movement, you can make Ivy Leaguers ashamed of their snobbish upbringing. With a strong invasion push you can make them blush every time you mention the Harvard Club.

At its worst, invasion of someone's past borders on blackmail. You make a discovery of territorial sensitivity—a drugaddict sister, a criminal father—and allude to it guardedly when you want to exert manipulative pressure. Everyone's face bears the shadows of some dark memory. Reach for those shadows and store them away for the time when you want to cast them across disputed territory to hide your manipulative advances.

Playing the Prophet

Predictive threats—dire warnings about the future—are a particularly virulent type of fear arousal. In a competitive organization your presence may suggest that you are going to stand where someone else wants to stand next month or next year, either in position or in favor. You should watch to see what positions people around you are expecting to occupy so that you can predict their attitudes and responses. Everyone wants to be a prophet. Since you are seeking dominance, you must be the most confident and accurate prophet around. That way you control the future by shaping it in *your* terms for *your* purpose because once an event is predicted it is more likely to occur.

Any predicted change in the status quo—positive or negative—can be an effective threat. Politicians are skillful at negative prophecy. They present graphs analyzing past trends to show that disaster will occur unless certain legislation is passed. Unless the federal government covers New York City's debts, economic chaos will result for the entire nation—so metropolitan prophets foretell.

Industry too is glad to play the prophet of doom to protect its interests. Protective tariffs, government subsidies, tax breaks, and innumerable other advantages are demanded so that the economy will not collapse within the next ten years.

Any threat of disruption to the status quo makes people shudder. No one wants to move from a comfortable position to chaos.

Suppose an office reorganization is planned. Someone is likely to be without a job. Suppose you are going to move the furniture. Somebody is going to be without a window. No area of activity is too small or too large to be used for predictive manipulation. The future, because of its uncertainty, is a constant threat. Changing prices, changing management, changing buying patterns, changing social attitudes—any of these can be called on as proof that what you recommend will save people from the disaster that your opponents are working to bring about.

"Futurism" is the big word in industrial planning. "The Russians will get you if you don't." "The environment will get you if you don't." "Overpopulation will get you if you don't." Cosmic threats abound for the shrewd manipulator. And why not? Unless you point people in the right direction with threats, others will use the same tools on you for their own destructive purposes.

You develop prophetic threats by the same method that you develop others: by finding out the central fears of your subjects and shaping your prophecies to them. If your prophecy is directed toward the entire organization, you may want to put it in written form. As with all written threats, you must be careful because you are making a permanent record. In the area of prophecy especially, your written words can come back to haunt you.

Most of the time, it is best to keep your threats spoken. Then, when the future is upon you and somebody points out that your prophecy failed, all you have to do is say, "Oh, no, you didn't understand at the time. People never do. It has worked out exactly as I predicted." Remind them of the Trojan princess Cassandra, who was doomed to speak the truth without being understood. You and Cassandra have a lot in common. Nobody ever understands what you are saying until it is too late to do anything about it.

When you have found your victim's deepest fear, couch your prophecy in as ambiguous a way as possible. The best prophets know the virtue of vague generalization. Play upon a general fear of economic collapse, global warfare, dwindling markets, giving the impression of dire consequences without being exact or specific.

Then choose a time when your subject is most dejected— late afternoon at coffee perhaps, when he is only half listening —and startle him awake with your dire prediction. You can tell he is trapped when he suddenly sits up and says, "What did you say?'' His eyes glaze over with fear, and he asks for more lurid details.

Be stingy with those details. Move on to another topic as if you don't recognize his anguish. Several days later he will return to the prophecy. By that time you will have something else to add to your future threat, and you can keep your victim in a state of fearful siege as long as necessary.

The prophetic threat is commonly used in politics. You can hear it on practically any newscast of Washington investigations or hearings. By studying these obvious examples you can learn to develop a subtle approach that serves you far better than the idle prophecies of politicians.

Getting Physical

Like the territorial threat, the physical threat may be either intentional or unintentional. Take the matter of height. We seldom realize that our presence may be a threat to the very short or the very tall. Short people sometimes try to compensate by commenting on the difference. They assume, rightly, that if they name it they can control it. Mentioning their stature before someone else gives them an advantage and makes people of normal height feel physically awkward. The implication is that people of normal height are at fault for discriminating against abnormal types.

To become the aggressor, you initiate the physical intimidation. Height, weight, baldness, bad skin, beard—any distinguishing physical characteristic can be a basis for your threats. You don't have to go in for overkill. You can throw a bald man off his psychic balance simply by running your hands through your long, glossy hair while talking to him. You can make a beardless man feel naked by stroking your beard in a meditative fashion. Such ploys catch people off balance and give you momentary advantage.

Physical gestures and comments about appearance do not have to be derogatory. A compliment can achieve the same purpose. People who have spent a lot of time dressing become self-conscious if you compliment them on something they haven't considered. Suppose, for example, a woman has color-coordinated her bag, shoes, and dress carefully; her belt does not match. You compliment the belt.

Self-consciousness about sexual differences can also be exploited. Women can intimidate men by becoming suddenly ultrafeminine or assuming a "masculine" role. A woman can take over the dominant position in a group of men by telling a loud, bawdy tale. This sex-reversal technique threatens the men and gives the woman an advantage.

Whenever I think of male-female threat situations, I think of Barbara Jane, a plump, dowdy woman of 30. She was a sales representative for electrical products. At a convention of wholesalers—mostly men—she demonstrated the superiority of an electric popcorn popper by contrasting it with the old method of cooking popcorn in a pan. For the occasion she wore skin-tight slacks and a sweater just a little tighter. When she began showing how to shake the popcorn in the old way she shimmied like a go-go dancer.

She glanced down, hesitated, and then went bravely on, shaking her popcorn with vigorous abandon. The 75 wholesalers in the audience blushed and shuffled their feet. Barbara Jane gritted her teeth and struggled through to her conclusion: "So you see how much smoother and easier our electric model can do it."

After she finished writing up orders, I heard the men commenting, "That poor woman. Did you ever see such a show!" They were torn between laughter and enbarrassment for Barbara Jane. But they all gave her a large order because she had worked so hard to do the right thing by her product. They were sure she would never wear a sweater like that again for the popcorn demonstration.

I was a little more suspicious. "Barbara Jane," I asked her when the crowd had moved on and she was putting the sheaf of new orders in her briefcase, "did you wear that sweater on purpose?"

She patted her briefcase and smiled. "I keep a record of the places where I haven't done that trick before. It works only one time for each group of salesmen."

Barbara Jane is admirable because she knew how to use her disadvantages to advantage. She could have demonstrated her popcorn popper in a tailored dress and gone home with a blank order book; but she decided that men with money pity a fat girl and admire endurance in the face of obstacles. The result was that her breasts posed an undefinable physical threat to the maleness of her audience.

Physical confrontation can also be used to gain a dominant position. You notice that whenever you meet an associate in a hall or doorway you have to move around him. You soon realize it is a symbolic refusal to give ground. He is trying to gain control by physical confrontation.

When one 6'6" hulk tried this with me, I realized the attempt to gain advantage. For several days he blocked the door to the general office area when I wanted to pass through. The next day I wore a pair of heavy hiking boots with ridged soles. When I saw him blocking my path, jubilation surged through me. I walked straight at him and planted my foot on top of his unprotected instep. He shouted and jumped back. I looked surprised and said, "Oh, excuse me." We've had a better understanding since then.

A verbal blow sometimes works as well as a physical encounter. If someone tries the symbolic blocking, move closer and say, "If you are going to loiter, why don't you do it in your office, where people aren't working?" Since the point of these physical confrontations is to establish dominance, you should not use them unless you are pretty sure they will work. And never undertake physical confrontation needlessly; do it only when you need it for conquest.

Image Breaking

We maintain our projected image by characteristic gestures and attitudes that form our *pose*. A threat to this public image is a powerful kind of manipulation. Sometimes it does not take much to shatter a person's public image and gain control.

Edgar saw himself as a shrewd, high-powered government official. He wore his Phi Beta Kappa key on a chain across his vest and a war decoration in his buttonhole. This self-assured dignitary was thrown into a shivering emotional state whenever he saw Bart, because Bart always shouted "Hi, Eddie! By breaking through the distinguished image Edgar was trying to project on his professional life, Bart touched Edgar's emotional vitals.

The incongruous juxtaposition of an imposed image over a projected one can be a powerful threat. If people want to be seen as witty logicians, treat them as if they were dull, tongue-tied idiots. Ask them to be clearer in their definitions, not quite so cumbersome in their reports. The distortion of their projected image throws them off balance and gives you the advantage.

Accusations of inconsistency also work for image breakers. You ask naively if this serious manager is the same person who acted such a fool at the office party. When an associate plays the research scholar, remind him that he got most of his information from a TV special your children told you about at dinner.

To protect yourself against pose breakers, you must cultivate a multifaceted personality that does not depend on pose. If you play the competent, unpretentious person who occasionally makes a mistake, you will be invulnerable to pose challengers. If you are the first to recognize your inconsistencies and laugh at them, the manipulators will have no ammunition to snipe with.

A sense of humor is the best defense against threats. When someone threatens you with territorial aggression, physical confrontation, or any other fear tactic—laugh. Out of your deep-seated security let a friendly, comfortable guffaw destroy the threat and bounce back on the threatener.

Carrying out Threats

So far in this chapter we have talked about techniques for creating fear through the manipulation of threat situations. Usually the threat is enough to activate the fear and achieve your purpose. Once in a while, though, you will have to follow through, either because the threat was hastily devised and did not create enough fear to incapacitate your manipulatee or because your subject was too naive to recognize it.

Whatever the reason, you have two choices when your victim does not respond to your threat. You can defuse the threat quietly so that your victim is unaware that it was ever made, or you can follow through. If the threat has been a private one, it is usually easier to pretend that it never existed at all, because implementing a threat usually carries some danger to your own position and is always time consuming.

At times, though, you must determine the most efficient and graceful way to show that your threat was not an empty gesture. When this time comes, examine your own position carefully. Do you want to use formal, organizational force to fulfill the threat, or would it be better to come at the rebellious manipulatee by more underhanded means?

If you use your superior position and go through channels to chastise or fire the person, then you have used up part of your own power as a manager. You cannot get the reputation in the organization for being a vindictive person. Whenever possible, it is better to give an unexpected twist to the threat and keep it away from official notice. If the threat you have made is as ambiguous as a good one should be, then you have a sizable degree of flexibility. You can withdraw your support in department meetings, resort to slander, or, by almost any other form of manipulation, indicate that you are now exerting the actual pressure that was previously just threatened.

Watchful Willie

Willie, who laughs now about how he rose to his present

position as a supergrade Washington executive, used several kinds of threat along the way.

JONES: So you think the threat can be useful for manipulating people?

WILLIE: One of the best. When I was young, I saw that most people I worked with were afraid of something—authority, disgrace, financial failure. You name it; they shivered at it. So I started naming it. I'd watch people who were gunning for me, and I'd see them wince at something. Then I knew where to dig in. I had threatening words for everybody I worked with. If people got out of line, I'd turn the conversation around to the words that made them cringe.

JONES: Can you remember any examples?

WILLIE: Sure. There was this one guy who was a real bastard. Nobody could get along with him. He was a tough one all right. Once I heard him talking to his wife on the phone. Then I heard something different. It was all "sugar" and "honey."

I didn't know why then, but I could tell he was scared of her. Little by little, I experimented. I used stories to draw a bead on his fear. I told a story about a husband who had been unfaithful to his wife. That tough guy turned pale. I'll swear he did! I never got a more pronounced response.

After that, I didn't have any trouble with him. I'd drop a hint that I understood, and he was always grateful to me for understanding his weakness. See, he couldn't help chasing other women, and his wife knew it. I had as much control over that guy as if he'd been unfaithful to me.

JONES: Doesn't a threat like that make people hate you? You say this man's grateful, but I should think he'd never want to see you again.

WILLIE: I'm not in business to be loved; but as it turns out the people I threaten don't hate me. Most of them are afraid of me, but that's different. They know I'm somebody to look out for, and they respect me. Being a mealymouth doesn't get you anything but a kick in the butt. I've got control, and people like those in control.

Besides, I never use a threat unless I have to. Only a fool would threaten without a good reason. I'm gentle. I don't put on enough pressure to break an arm, just enough to get my way.

JONES: Have you ever had to threaten directly—I mean in writing or speaking?

WILLIE: Sure. When somebody puts the pressure on me, I pick up the telephone and hint at possible horrors awaiting them. You never get anywhere in business if you petition people. You've got to threaten them with something they're really scared of. Usually all I have to do is say that I'll send a letter to a higher authority unless I get my way immediately. Most people are scared of their superiors, so I offer to take the matter up a notch or two. They don't want to rock the boat, so they compromise before I have to write anything. And compromise is usually what I wanted in the first place.

JONES: So you don't feel that using threats is playing dirty?

WILLIE: Hell, no! That's the way the system works. Put the pressure on and you get things done. Anybody who tells you different ought to be in church, not government.

JONES: Have you ever been threatened?

WILLIE: Plenty. And the only protection is to threaten louder. That's what I do. I'll go one step closer to the brink than anybody else here because to tell you the truth I don't really give a damn anyway.

JONES: That may be the best way to win—not care about winning.

WILLIE: Don't get me wrong. I care a lot about winning. What

I don't care about is what anybody else can do to hurt me. I've been hurt so much that I've developed an immunity to threats. Nobody can do anything to me much worse than what's been done to me already. So I walk through the plague sure of survival.

JONES: You've done very well so far. And with the way you use threats you'll probably continue to succeed as well as survive. I hope so.

8

SEX

Hitting Below the Belt

PEOPLE who love power sometimes enjoy exerting it sexually as well as professionally. When they have grown dull and jaded with success, they supplement the thrills of power play with sexual play. This erotic proclivity makes such people easy marks for sexual manipulation. Many middle-aged executives who are accustomed to winning enjoy the challenge of testing their charms now and then. These tests help them maintain a semblance of sexual alertness for the sake of their egos. And no one who undertakes sexual manipulation should ever feel that the final bedding is where the action is. Stimulation comes mostly from the chase.

In the area of sex the personal world impinges on the public one. Faced daily with a mass of dehumanized person-objects to manipulate, managers flee in the opposite direction—toward sex, the most private, personal activity still available to them. Ironically, they usually look for it at the office, which they regard as the cosmic center. Since they are themselves skilled manipulators by training and practice, they enjoy exercising these skills in the seduction process.

If you are aware of this tendency in business situations, you can find out your subject's deepest sexual yearnings and play to them with bawdy abandon. You don't have to surrender

your innocence in order to manipulate erotically. As a matter
of fact, it is usually wiser to hold on to it; it's probably part of
your irresistible charm.

And in today's business world that charm can be either male
or female. Any man or woman, at any age, who is sincerely
committed to manipulation theory can find delightfully stimulating ways to use sex to gain control over others. As we move
through this chapter, we will see that sex is omnipresent in the
musk-laden air of modern businesses.

What Turns Them On

The personal sacrifices young executives of both sexes
make in order to advance quickly intensify their sexual drives.
The feeling of urgency, which motivated their climb to success, also makes them want to get as much sex as possible in
the time left them. Driven by unfulfilled fantasies, they grow
frustrated, spending more and more time in centerfold medita-
tion. To such unsatisfied people a dirty joke can raise interest
as quickly as a lifted skirt. The slightest sexual hint elicits a
violently prurient response.

With people so easily aroused it is best to play a waiting
game. Watch their interests, their eye movements in crowds,
and suggest by your sympathetic responses that you approve
of their sexual orientation, or at least accept it as the best
solution for them. Whatever their choice—marriage, infidelity,
orgiastic license—you have to be understanding. Many worshiping subordinates set the example for this kind of *sympathetic sexuality*. They come to believe what they condone and
apologize for in their bosses with some such statement as
"Considering what he has to go through, he's doing the best he
can."

Sympathetic sexuality begins by establishing the dominant
sexual preferences of your subject. You don't need to do an
in-depth Freudian analysis of your manipulatee's sexuality;
you can find out enough for your manipulation simply by en-

gaging in casual conversation about favorite pastimes—hobbies, TV shows, magazines. These should give you enough points to chart a fairly accurate graph of sexual preferences. Then you can begin your manipulation by playing to your subject's deepest sexual desires. Here is how it works.

To decorate the bare rudeness of our sexual urgency, we each construct a fantasy that we run inside our heads to beautify the sexual act. This can be a spectacular epic with casts of thousands or an intimate bedroom comedy, depending on our early models. In either case, the potential mating scene requires supporting actors in addition to the two leading roles. Sex, you see, is not just one on one, but a group affair. Adultery wouldn't be as much fun without a disapproving spouse close by; shocked parents make the first sexual games more exciting.

In preparing for your part in the Sympathetic Sexuality Show, you look at the required cast for the various types of sex shows and then step easily into the role of your choosing—go-between, authoritarian elder, lewd friend, shocked observer. It makes little difference whether you are playing the role for a male or a female executive. Earlier, when women's roles in society were different from those of men, differences in sexual desires were also assumed. Now that women are doing the same jobs as men in the business world, they tend to respond sexually much as men do. The following scenarios are therefore equally appropriate for manipulating female executives, although the stories are told in the old-fashioned masculine terms.

Many executives are turned on by pallid helplessness. They like to feel the strength of their superiority surging through them. Even in this age of the liberated woman, they are slow converts to sexual equality. They are easily identified by their favorite TV shows: *The Waltons* and *Little House on the Prairie.* They are romantics who believe in the triumph of justice in human affairs.

For this type, the sex fantasy to build on is *Camille.* The

French original and the Greta Garbo movie are mostly forgotten now, but the plot is still running in their heads. A beautiful woman, dying of tuberculosis, is desperately loved by a rich man whose family disapproves of the affair. The friends of the two lovers are divided in their allegiance to them, but the love continues right up to the glorious deathbed scene.

If you are a woman, you can control the Camille type by playing helpless. If you are a young man, you can approximate the fluttering helplessness of an elegant young swan in a trap. The supporting cast—the group that makes the sexual anticipation so poignant—is composed of the socially correct family and friends. If you are not suited to play Camille, you can become indispensable by being the just, conservative person your manipulatee needs to revolt against. Wanting to sleep with a helpless woman is only part of his sexual fantasy. He loves even more the strength that flows through him as he resists well-intentioned friends to cling to the object of his affection. Sex for him is a project, a commitment, a passion. Possessed of a wide idealistic streak, he would be horrified at the thought of actually consummating the sexual act. He prefers consumption to consummation.

Another common type is the aggressive sexualist. He saw *Gone with the Wind* six times, and his favorite TV shows are football games and hockey matches. He is a managerial Rhett Butler out to tame the flaming Scarlett. Weak women do not turn him on sexually. He wants someone who will bite and claw and kick. Like the Camille type, he is sexually positive; but he feels his sexual power through the resistance of his partners rather than through their helplessness.

To manipulate this type, women can play the office Scarlett. The more they reject their victim, the more desperately he wants to possess their souls. Male associates can play one of Scarlett's husbands or the charming Ashley Wilkes. They can also offer him jovial male companionship of the poker-playing, beer-guzzling sort that is part of the Rhett Butler mystique. For a novel approach, a man of the right sort can transcend sexual boundaries and take on the role of Miss Melanie, whose approval as a moral, upright person the bounder secretly needs for complete emotional fulfillment.

The aggressive sexualist responds well to dirty jokes and broad humor. He prides himself on his manipulative skill. He needs constant reassurance of his success, professional and sexual. This greediness for reassurance results in a pushy business approach. The best way to control him is to go along with his aggression until you can turn it aside for your own purpose.

A third type is the passive sexualist. His favorite TV show is *The Bionic Woman.* The powerful woman figure reassures him that he can do nothing to equal her accomplishments. These passivists sublimate their desires. They play chess, read *The New Yorker*, and never buy anything without consulting *Consumer Reports.*

The Bionic Woman types are inclined to be old-maidish, but they can be managed by pampering their sulkiness and humoring their humorlessness. A woman approaches these listless types with protective strength. She is the Great Mother, threatening them with punishment when they do wrong and rewarding them with a warm, soothing breast when they are hurt.

Men must be cautious in manipulating Bionic Woman types. If they try to play the same passive game, they will become threats, competing for the Great Mother's affection. With passivists, it is much better to play a contrasting, but supportive, sexual role. Ashley Wilkes, you remember, always thought Rhett Butler a remarkable man; and Rhett admired Ashley's purity, even when he was competing with him for Scarlett's love.

These three sexual types are only samples of the numerous ones you will come across as you interview candidates for sexual manipulation. You will be successful if you remember that you can play any one of several roles in their fantasies. In same-sex encounters, though, you are usually safest if you assume a basic character opposite.

Sexual Diagnosis

As you begin to recognize your subject's erotic propensities, you experiment gently to find exactly how to satisfy them most pleasantly. Some people enjoy feeling guilty about sex. For these guilt grabbers you may have to play a parental no-no role. You are the authority whose watchful eye they try to avoid. For those who prefer open lewdness, you take on the pimp role, introducing them to new fleshly pleasures.

When Floyd was transferred to a new section, everyone told him that he was working for an impossible woman. "Lois will castrate you the first week," they told him. "She won't have anyone but geldings working for her. The next time we see you, you'll be singing boy soprano. Good-by, manhood!"

Floyd's first unpleasant experiences with Lois reinforced everything people had told him. She dominated and slashed at every man in sight. Floyd began making mental notes about her. He remembered that everyone tended to see her in sexual —or antisexual—terms. Lois's hangup must be sexually derived, Floyd decided. He found out that she had been married three times and was presently divorced. She was probably not any happier than the poor men she misused on the job.

Floyd's diagnosis of Lois's problem: she needed a good man, and soon. Not ready to provide the stud service himself, he looked around the office, only to discover that she had debilitated all the men in his section and most of the men she worked with in other sections as well. Lois had to have someone to treat her rougher than she treated the men around her.

As Floyd continued thinking about Lois, he began to see the mythic pattern that had to be imposed on the terrible working situation: he had to find someone for a starring role in *The Taming of the Shrew*.

Racking his brain for the right man, Floyd came up with Larry, an old friend who had been recently divorced and was quite lonely. Larry was unenlightened about the new position of women in the universe. He thought they should still be in the kitchen. Floyd told his wife he was going to have Lois and Larry over to dinner. "You're crazy," she said. "They'll tear each other to pieces."

"That might be fun to watch," Floyd said.

They did rip into each other before cocktails were finished. But they hated each other so much that they had to meet again to finish the fight. They began going out together, and eventually Larry proudly told Floyd that he had moved in at Lois's for an extended visit. "Nothing permanent, you understand. Just till I get her completely broken to the whip. Then I'll demand that she give up her job and marry me."

The result of Floyd's mating service was that Lois was so busy with fights at home that she became quite agreeable at work. Even though she sometimes damned Floyd for having introduced her to Larry, she felt a special gratitude for the way Floyd had enriched her life. She had never had so much fun at home before. She had finally found a man she could not dominate; she no longer had to test every man she met to see if he would break.

Older male executives sometimes suffer from decreasing sexual prowess. They respond well—and harmlessly—to rather flagrant sexual games. After a few initial experiments, women can feel free to flirt brazenly with them. Body contact —a brush of the hands, shoulders, breasts, or knees—is probably a safe form of manipulation. Men who want to manipulate an older male executive can add to discreet bodily contact vivid personal narratives and allusions to the legendary amorous powers of their manipulatee.

Older female executives often have a romantic streak. With them, intimate flattery stirs a nostalgic sexual spark. A younger man manipulating these women has to be passive in his sex role. Once he tacitly indicates his sexual interest, he must let the executive be the aggressor. Tender, sentimental admiration for older female executives is usually safe, even when it is outwardly spurned.

One of my first superiors in the Army was a WAC lieutenant. I was 19 and she was an ancient 35. I was incapable of imposing any pattern on our relationship because I was only semiconscious most of the time from fear and adolescent sexual confusion. Luckily, that was exactly what turned the lieutenant on. Her maternal urges had been thwarted in the Army while her erotic experiences were legion. In a largely masculine, military world she was psychologically aware enough to use me to balance her personal needs.

The relationship was good for both of us because she gave me the psychic shelter I needed without threatening my budding sexuality. As with any mother-son relationship, of course, there were some slight erotic overtones that were pleasing too.

When I later began to develop theories of sexual manipulation, I used this one as a model. I saw that at each age people need others for a variety of sexual appetites. Through manipulative dexterity we can shape ourselves to these needs and keep our subjects at just the right level of physical excitement. Had I been much older than 19, I would have had to take a more active role in satisfying my WAC's desires. There are enough roles to go around for all of us, though, and auditioning for the parts can be fun at any age.

Again, do not think that because you are of the same sex as your manipulatee that you cannot use sexual manipulation. Sometimes we understand the sexual needs of our own sex better than those of the opposite sex. By recalling earlier attitudes of and experiences with others of our sex, we can collect a sizable storehouse of props to delight and excite those of both sexes.

The only danger in same-sex manipulation is jealousy. Older executives envy the vigor of the young. Such jealousy can be allayed by subtle comments about the advantages of experience and mature charm. An occasional naive question about sexual matters also puts an older manager in an expansive, reminiscent mood.

Both old and young are hungry to expand their sexual

knowledge. The manipulator should see each sexually based manipulation as a perpetual burlesque show in which dullness is avoided by a rapid change of acts. Compliments and grossness should be interwoven with shy blushes and hesitant withdrawals. Such shifts make the manipulatee pant with excitement and strive to penetrate the depths of your amorous nature.

Since you can never be sure of an executive's sexual orientation, you should be careful when you refer to various perversions. Do not touch a tender spot unless you have a special purpose. Let the people you are manipulating guide you to discussions of what interests them. If they are coy, respect their reserve—and watch carefully. Since people are insecure about the most innocuous sexual practices, you can gain control by sly allusions to abnormal sex drives. The forbidden always entices.

When you want to create a moment of weakness so that you can swing someone into line, a sudden reference to a perversion can be quite effective. Mention child molesting or the growing rate of voyeurism and you elicit a shiver from the most debauched subject. Sexual guilt persists for years, and while it lives it might as well be working for you.

The Freudian overtones in same-sex relationships are complex, but all you need to do is to discover your psychosexual relationship with people and then press on it. When they start groaning, take your pressure off.

Sex as we are thinking of it here is more than the physical act. It is the spark of physicality that ties two people together in some essential awareness. The sexual act can be the final expression of this throbbing awareness, but many highly sensual relationships do not culminate in a sexual encounter.

In many circles the taboos against same-sex relationships are so strong that you must be careful never to suggest the possibility of a direct sexual encounter. These taboos, though, make the urge for friendship and kinship all the stronger. Your knowledge of this urge gives you the advantage. You can manipulate for your own good and the greater happiness of your manipulatees, whose blood will course faster through their veins as a result of your secret sharing.

Sexual Indicators

Physical behavior is a subtle indicator of sexual attitudes. How do people stand and move as they talk to each other? What do they do with their hands? How much do they reach out or touch the person to whom they are talking? Sexual yearning and sexual aggression are behind many of these physical actions.

As you observe your subjects, note the positions they take when they talk with others. Then imitate the postures and gestures of the people with whom they feel most at ease. This simple act will help you become one of the trusted people in their circle.

Until you have learned how far you can go with a subject, minimum physical expression is advisable. Reactions to physical contact vary among ethnic and social groups. A gesture of jovial friendliness in one group is sexual assault in another. Minimum physical response is safe to begin with because it leaves you plenty of time for playing your subjects until they're exhausted. Your response should also be guided by how much you can imitate other people's behavior and yet remain yourself. Your ultimate purpose is to control the physical relationship so that you manipulate your subject in the direction you want.

In the narrowest sense, this kind of physical manipulation is not sexual, but it is derived from sexual origins. Physical contact is often a substitute for sexual gratification. You can go a long way in playing the *substitution game* if you let body play replace bed play. While you prepare your subjects for the kill, your sensuality can keep them thrilled.

Body play. Since sex is such a strong drive, most people avoid boredom by playing interpersonal sexual games with their bodies. Depending on your purpose, you can delight or upset a member of the opposite sex by using your arms or hands for seemingly accidental caresses. The slightest brush can be the subtle suggestion of sexual awareness. A woman can throw a man into a panic by letting her hair brush lightly against his as she leans over him to get a pencil. A man can threaten a woman by bringing his cheek up in line with hers so that if she turns her head it is in kissing position.

Your body play becomes sensual when you yourself think sensual thoughts. Don't overdo it, or you will frighten the timid rabbit back into hiding. Any object can become a sex object if you use it symbolically. A pencil stroked gently with the tip of your fingers or a door knob rubbed casually with the palm of your hand can be a bright spot in your manipulatee's otherwise dull day.

Word play. Words also cultivate a mood of sensuality that excites and unites you with your manipulatee. Talk about the file drawers as though they were sex objects to be violated and your filing clerk will file as he has never filed before. You can transform the cosmos into a huge sexual metaphor to be exploited with language. Everything that protrudes is phallic and everything cavernous is vaginal. You don't want to be too obvious, but you can inject a double meaning into practically everything you say if you're thinking sex as you say it.

Suppose you are a younger man working for an older one. He is conservative and distant in his relationship. You want to bring some life into the situation; sexual manipulation is a possible solution. Suggestive sexual word play will stimulate him without offending him. Let the project you are working on become female. Speak of it as feminine and gradually let it become a desired sex object. Soon you are both saying, "We'll give her the hots" and "Let's knock her up." When you both are thinking of your work as an object of seduction, you share a secret sex language that draws you together and enriches your relationship.

Outward appearances. The clothes people wear also indicate their degree of sexuality. There are three useful style classifications for purposes of manipulation: readys, maybe-laters, and nevers.

Readys are the most sensitive to changes in style. Men of this breed wear their jeans tightest or loosest, depending on the prevailing pattern for the jeans set. Their lapels and ties are the widest or narrowest because they care what's right right now. The higher their style, the more physically responsive they are. Obviously, they think about their bodies a lot—and probably about other people's bodies in relation to them.

These flesh flashers are immediately responsive to flattery. They treasure their projected image and will gladly compromise their self-image to win the approbation of others. They respond to bawdiness and enjoy physical contact. They are not prudish and are suspicious of those who are. To them, any sign of reserve suggests snobbery or, even worse, hypocrisy. They assume the rest of the world is as interested in flesh as they are but just won't admit it.

Maybe-laters are less concerned with their appearance. Women of this type will not change their dress length for fashion's sake, but will wear good clothes a long time. Men in this group will not throw away a jacket because the lapels are not the right width and may even wear brown socks with a blue suit.

These people respond more to wit and logic than to flattery. They enjoy sophisticated conversation but are easily managed with a straightforward greeting, a direct glance, and a minimum of physical contact. A firm handshake is about all the fleshly experience they can endure without self-consciousness. They are shy initially in direct sexual discussions; but once they open up they are more truly passionate than the readys, who sometimes advertise more than they have to offer.

Nevers are recognized by their unmatched socks, strange color combinations, and total disregard for style. They are sometimes buttoned up wrong and look as if their clothes fell on them while they were walking under a tree. They are easy to deal with because they are oblivious to physical possibilities. You can slap them on the back, shake their hand, or rub their fanny, and they will go on talking with a distant look in their eyes. You may be able to talk them around to your point of view, but it is almost impossible to manipulate them physically except by pushing them out of the way.

With everyone, even nevers, dress style is the key to sexuality. Your subjects' secret drives and self-images are displayed everyday for you in what they are wearing. All you need to do is to read the signs.

Sexual Conversation

Once you have located your subject on the sexuality scale, you can devise a winning approach. Many executives, frustrated by heavy paperwork and a nonphysical business grind, strive against their bondage with vivid sexual fantasies. Unless these people are totally repressed, direct allusions to your personal exploits can be useful in manipulating them. If you share a few of your sexual experiences or fantasies in intimate tones, you can develop a camaraderie that carries over into business relationships as well.

Be ready to listen too. These people sometimes find the recounting of an adventure more erotic than the adventure itself. Contribute just enough of your own sexual tales to keep the conversation going, but never let your adventures overshadow theirs.

Your age relationship should help you determine the right approach here. One supervisor, who had little time for communication with his staff, spent 20 minutes every Monday morning with the young male Xerox operator. The staff investigated, expecting to find out the worst. They discovered that the boy went to pornographic movies every weekend and recounted the movie of the week for the boss's benefit on Monday mornings.

Some staff members were offended that a man who was too busy for them had time for movie reports. One of them, Don, turned the situation to his advantage. At first he sent the Xerox operator to the boss's office with papers for the boss to sign. A few months later Don had a stag party for some friends and invited the boss to see the movie. Now Don gets invited in on Mondays along with the office boy.

More sophisticated, sexually aware types are ill at ease with sexual conversations or pornography, but bawdy tales and lewd references sometimes build a closeness with them. The sharing of a funny story—dirty or not—cultivates a sense of community that people with any degree of physicality enjoy.

Whatever their degree of sexuality, your manipulatees have some sexual hangups. These irrational responses are frequently a clue to some of their behavior patterns. The man who flies into hysterical rage may not be mad at you. An unresolved Oedipus complex is expressing itself. He's really frustrated at not being able to marry his mother. The woman who slashes a male associate to pieces verbally may actually be wanting to castrate him to satisfy her Electra complex.

The original parent-child relationship, if you can discover it, will often help you in your manipulation. When an older man spoke firmly to an executive at the end of a long conference, the executive burst into tears and ran out of the room. He realized later that it was an exact repetition of scenes when his authoritarian father had reprimanded him at the dinner table.

Careful observation will show you latent tendencies toward exhibitionism, voyeurism, child molesting, and other sexual problems. If you can spot these tendencies, you will gain great manipulative power. How you use these psychosexual states depends on your long-range plan for manipulation, but knowledge of these unconscious psychic states can give you a sharp instrument for any form of sexual manipulation.

Last Resort

An affair is so explosive that it frequently has uncontrollable consequences for the manipulator. Its instability makes it a cumbersome and ineffectual manipulative device. Once you have started an affair with your subject, you have changed from a professional to a personal relationship and submitted to control.

The woman who feels she is gaining an advantage by sleeping with the boss may enjoy a few months of triumph in the office. But her co-workers will continue to manipulate the manager in a variety of ways after she has been fired—either by a disappointed, satiated boss or by an angry wife. Even if she marries the boss, she loses her advantage: some other woman in the office will take her role as controller of the married man.

Anticipation of an affair, though, is a strong manipulative device. Skillful manipulators use physicality to suggest a deep sexual longing with the romantic overtones of unfulfilled desire. Speaking only with the body, they create an exciting, pleasing intimacy. People of either sex can manipulate sensually so that they hint at mysterious longing that someday may find gratification.

Sexuality is composed partly of guilt, partly of anticipation. The combination should be maintained in a delightfully mixed state. To keep a good mix, you have to avoid too many private moments with your subject. Although a certain amount of intimacy is necessary, you are unwise to sustain long, solitary periods together. A semipublic relationship suits sexual manipulation best. Sometimes you are alone with each other in the office, but the urgency of business—a phone call, an appointment—should always draw you away when the possibility of gratification arises.

Looking back over what you have learned about sexuality, you see that it assumes an interest in the flesh. You, as a manipulator, must suppress such interest when you are on the job. Unless you can control your sexual urges, you are likely to become the victim of others who will take advantage of your sexual longing. If you place fleshly titillation above the joys of manipulation, you will have some good times perhaps, but you will not succeed as a manipulator. Be sure the roles are not reversed so that you become subject rather than master.

Swirly Shirley and Ready Eddie

Of the many executives I talked to who used sexual manipulation in their jobs, Shirley and Eddie were the most successful. They also had a more stable home life than most of the others. That stability may be a cause or a result of their professional success. I suspect that domestic harmony contributes to control at work. Shirley and Eddie were not seeking sexual gratification away from home.

SHIRLEY: Don't you miss your family, being away from home so much, Dr. Jones? Do you ever bring them along?

JONES: No. The children are in school, and my wife teaches piano. But tell me about yourself. Do you, as a professional woman, a wife, and a mother, have any trouble balancing all these jobs?

SHIRLEY: No. I've always had lots of energy, and I think it's good for the children to learn to do things for themselves.

JONES: Why did you ask me right away about my family? So I'd ask about yours?

SHIRLEY: Actually, I don't talk much about my family or myself. I'm more interested in knowing about other people's private lives. Somehow it helps me understand them in business relationships.

JONES: What did you find out about me when I told you I didn't take my family along on these trips?

SHIRLEY: One answer doesn't tell me a lot. A few more questions and I could have found out whether you're happily married or on the prowl. Then I could have known whether to be easy and relaxed with you or on my guard.

JONES: What made you decide to open up?

SHIRLEY: Since you're only here for two weeks, it doesn't make much difference.

JONES: You mean you don't need to stake me out for manipulation?

SHIRLEY: Oh, I'll probably do that anyway from force of

habit. The way we're sitting has changed since we started talking. We're treating each other as people now rather than as potential sex objects.

JONES: Do you find yourself thinking much about physical relationships with the men you work with? As a woman in upper management, and as attractive as you are, do you have to do a lot of refusing?

SHIRLEY: No more than I want to. I've learned a lot in the past ten years. I can turn men off sexually before they know they've started. It hasn't always been that way. I had a bad experience with my first boss. I was just out of college, and he was 40, distinguished and successful. He came at me, and I was flattered. Then I heard from the other women that he went after every new female. I decided that I was going to be the predator instead of the prey from then on. I've developed all kinds of sexual games to use on male executives when I need to.

JONES: Does your husband care?

SHIRLEY: Not at all. We laugh about the fools I make of them. Lately I've used sex not to lure, but to threaten. With so much emphasis on advancing women's positions, I've played the suppressed-minority thing for all it's worth.

JONES: But before that, did you ever have an unfortunate sexual encounter at work?

SHIRLEY: No. I've always been in control. Whether men are married or single, gay or straight, I have developed techniques to keep them in line till I need them.

JONES: How does that affect your relationships with other women executives?

SHIRLEY: I manage women the same way. The stupid ones I fix up with the men they get sweet on. I listen to their love stories with a sympathetic ear. But I also parade stern authority when I have to. Most women collapse before that traditionally masculine characteristic. I'd say I get along with women as well as with men, and for the same reason: I'm alert to their sexual attitudes.

JONES: So since your first boss you have never gotten emotionally involved?

SHIRLEY: Not the way you mean it. I have warm and open relationships with most of the people around here. I like almost everybody so I don't feel bad turning people in the direction they ought to be turned. If I didn't believe it was for their good as well as mine, I'd think again about playing with them the way I do. I don't hurt people. I help them.

JONES: Well, you've helped me understand the way sexual manipulation works. You come at people through honest, loving concern and a sincere interest in the flesh.

SHIRLEY: I guess that's right.

Like Shirley, Eddie enjoyed telling me how he manipulated people through their sexual interests.

JONES: I've been talking to some of the women around here about the part sex consciousness plays in their professional relationships. Do you think sex-related matters have any effect on your career?

EDDIE: If you mean do I ever think about it, yes. Most of the men I work with can be kept friendly if you drop a filthy joke on them every day or two. Of course, you have to be careful. There are prudes who are offended by bawdy stories. With them I play the clean-mouthed saint.

JONES: You don't have trouble working with both kinds?

EDDIE: Not at all. I don't try to impose my ideas about sex on the people I work with. I stopped trying to save souls shortly after my third-grade revival. I just try to get along with whatever kind of people I'm around. You don't get very far being closed-minded. I talk abortion with one guy, "right to life" with another. I'm foul-mouthed or prudish. I reflect the taboos of the person I'm with.

JONES: Do you think everybody else does too?

EDDIE: Hardly anybody. That's what gives me an advantage.

Most people are very sneaky about sex. The guy who kept telling me how much he hated homosexuals eventually made a pass at me. There was no way around that one. I realized too late that his eagerness to condemn was a cover-up for his approach. When I didn't respond with scorn to his condemnation of homosexuals my tolerance made his expectations swell.

JONES: So how do you two get along now?

EDDIE: Just fine. I patted his cheek and told him I liked him a lot, but not that way. Once you settle things with people of either sex, you can move on to more solid relationships. The gay guy can still get a little jealous of me, but I keep it under control. He has plenty of his own kind around here.

JONES: How about women?

EDDIE: I play up to them. They expect it, and like everyone they need flattery and attention. Things get pretty drab for us all sometimes.

JONES: How did you get so aware of these sexual attitudes?

EDDIE: I keep my eyes open and my fly closed. I don't get involved emotionally. The saddest people are the ones who try to satisfy their sexual needs with quick grabs and fast talk. I'm ready for fun, but my way.

9

PRESSURE

Building Up Steam

IF YOU are around any office very long you'll hear somebody say, "We'll just have to lean on him a little." Leaning consists of bringing pressure to bear so that people move in the direction you want them to go. You're less likely to get burned from escaping steam if you know the kinds of pressures that build up.

Pressures are inevitable when people work together in a competitive situation. Frequently the pressures are undirected, unrecognized, and therefore unconstructive. They push this way and that, causing irritation and bad feeling. Recognize these pressures and keep your hand on the gauges, and you can keep those around you simmering for a long time.

Take a typical pressure situation. You are working on a committee to draft a proposal for a long-range employee parking plan. The members of the committee have different attitudes and backgrounds. One is a union representative; another is a professional; a third is from the finance department. These three generate steam at the meeting before they speak because each has built-in professional antagonisms.

In addition, they feel that their contributions to the organization are not appreciated. They suspect that their worth as individuals is being scorned by the other members of the committee. They also know that they are functioning not just as individuals but as representatives of a group to which they feel loyalty and responsibility.

This example shows the two kinds of pressures in any business situation: *existing pressure* and *created pressure.* In the example the existing pressure is the emotional tension created by professional antagonisms. This pressure alone will probably give you enough manipulative power to get your own way. Once you see the steam pouring from the committee members' mouths, you can play their antagonisms against one another. In your conversation during the meeting you can regulate the pressure by emphasizing or minimizing the differences in attitude.

Outside the committee you must see clearly the point of view of each member and remain open to it—not so open, of course, as to befog your own purpose. With your continued openness you can retain control of the pressure gauges, because you alone are still communicating with everyone. The others have stopped listening to each other.

At times the existing pressure is so powerful that you may want to bottle it up and continue with created pressure that you can manage more safely. For example, you can pull strings with individual members of the committee or appeal to greed or legality. In each case, you build up new pressures for the occasion. These pressures are covered in detail later in the chapter.

The trouble with pressure is that it shifts under your touch. Sometimes, as in the example of the parking committee, emotional pressure already exists in a situation. At other times the emotional pressure has to be built up for the occasion. You have to "create" emotions that don't yet "exist."

This slipperiness of types should not deter you from making a careful analysis of the situation. Prepare a checklist with two columns. In one column record the pressures that you see existing in the situation. In the other column list the created pressures appropriate for use. Keep the checklist nearby as you begin your pressure manipulation.

Legal Pressure

The most obvious kind of pressure in business is legal pressure. In extreme cases you may have to resort to lawyers; but this method of leaning is expensive and time-consuming, and is not guaranteed to succeed. One man spent three years fighting a legal battle to keep a trailer court out of his neighborhood. The developer put up the trailers in violation of local zoning laws. At the end of three years, with a little political pressure on the right zoning-board members, the owner of the trailer park managed to make his illegal trailers legal, leaving the homeowner out his legal fees and in a lot of pain.

The threat of legal process is often more useful than the process itself. By combining threat and pressure you come up with a powerful control technique. The authority-oriented executive is frightened by the thought of class-action suits and malpractice suits. Even though you may have nothing to gain from initiating such a suit, the suggestion that you might do so is enough to start the pressure building in your manipulatee.

One physician, who had always assumed that his malpractice insurance covered everything, seemed immune to legal pressure. Then the budget officer at the hospital pointed out that he was still open to civil prosecution in his financial dealings, which were not covered by his professional insurance. The physician was so frightened by this picture of financial ruin that he willingly agreed to a billing change that increased the budget officer's control.

The appeal to law is only the most visible form of legal pressure. Legalistic thinking is at the heart of much executive behavior. Tables of organization, lines of authority, and duty distribution come under the general heading of legal pressure. Every time you assign someone a task, you are leaning on implicit legality for compliance. Your daily performance at work is a trained response to the continuous pressure of your· "legal" job description.

If you take this ordinary, accepted pressure and make it

visible, you can regulate tensions to suit your purpose. When people are working hard at a task that is only tangential to their assigned duties, you can gain their gratitude and friendship by saying, "You know, you don't really have to do that job. It's not part of your responsibility." This kindly pressure relief gets you a lot of good will, even when you have no *legal* control over people's actions.

More often, you will want to increase the pressure on people by challenging their performance. Either they are usurping someone else's designated decision-making function or they are not fulfilling their own duties adequately. Many executives have been replaced after someone "suggested" that they were not functioning adequately in their legally assigned job.

Lower on the list of legal pressures are job regulations. Most organizations have either written or assumed roles. When you want to increase the pressure on your manipulatees, find some violation of a rule or tradition and bring it to light.

Pressures created by uncovering a breach in regulations can be exerted directly or indirectly. Sometimes you will want to work directly with the violators, letting them know that you are aware of their law breaking. At other times you will want to work indirectly, pointing out errors to superiors or associates. Once you know a subject's personality you can decide on the best approach. Guilt-ridden, well-meaning souls respond well to direct warnings, an approach akin to blackmail. Hardened-criminal types are best pressured indirectly, by making others aware of their violations.

Manipulation by legal pressure can backfire if you are not sensitive to group attitudes. If all the members of a group are looking for someone to break the law or are secretly bending the rules themselves, they may be pleased rather than disgusted with the rule breaker. Your pressure could push you into a corner where you are the sole advocate for regulations that others are longing to destroy. Legal pressure, like every other kind of manipulation, demands constant alertness to the environment in which it is used.

Emotional Pressure

Although emotions should be confined to private rather than public life, they often find their way into business situations. The totally rational executive is a rare creature. All of us have built-in likes and dislikes. We fear, resent, or hate people whose outlooks differ from ours. We like, pity, or love those we agree with. In our public lives these positive and negative emotions often interact to keep us in a constant state of tension. If we can control emotions in ourselves and others, we have a powerful manipulative tool.

The danger in working with emotions is that they are so difficult to predict. Two people, seemingly alike in background and temperament, will react in different ways to the same emotional pressure. One will break down and cry in anguish; the other will lash out with an uncontrolled wrath.

Generally, it is safest to use emotional pressure on people you know well. You should have an accurate chart of your subjects' temperaments before trying to create emotional pressure. You discover their susceptibilities to emotional stimuli by unobserved experiments in trivial matters. Here are some of the standard emotions you can count on.

Hatred. Playing on people's hatreds is one of the easiest ways to manage them. Everyone hates someone—a co-worker, a boss, the Democrats, the Communists. The list is infinite. In the chapter on prejudice we will investigate hatred in more detail; for the moment it is enough to say that hatred is one of the most lasting and dependable emotions. By comparison, positive emotions such as affection and pity are fleeting.

Once you have established hatred in your manipulatee, you can count on it and call it up at will. Mention the hated name, and you get an instantaneous reaction. By sharing the hater's emotion, you assure yourself of support and goodwill. For a long-term program, you can build up a collection of symbols around the hated object. Then you can control your victim's response by referring to one of the symbols rather than the hated object itself. The closer your symbol is to the horrible center, the stronger your victim's response will be.

Anger. A less trustworthy ally of hatred, and one of its products, is anger. It is momentary and arises from unpredictable sources. Still, if you can make your subjects mad, they are yours. Look for people who get so upset that they barge out of meetings or refuse to hear what is being said. Then use their reaction to your advantage.

You can arouse their anger yourself, but it is easier to play a waiting game. As you recognize the preliminary symptoms—squirming, hair-rubbing, reddening of the ears, twitching of the cheeks—you can anticipate the rage and include it in your program of manipulation.

People under the influence of wrath violate rational patterns of behavior. They vote against their own motions, knife their best friend, and recant all they hold dear. Unfortunately, since they are so irrational, you can't be sure of any predictable pattern to their anger. In one rage they may be traitorous to their friends; in the next they may cling to friendship desperately. The only thing you can be sure of is their inconsistency. That knowledge alone puts them, for that bright moment of fiery fury, in your complete control.

Fear. In the chapter on threats we talked about fear and the techniques for controlling it. Fear tactics are best used for curbing rather than stimulating action. Fearful people freeze up. Unless you are planning an economic-threat program, you cannot develop responsive actions out of fear.

Fear is a good pressure device when you want to scare your manipulatee into hiding. For example, at a meeting, you suspect that someone may come out in opposition to your program. You point out that the effects of this change on retirement benefits should be considered seriously. Retirement scares the fainthearted. With no exact data available, fearful souls withdraw into their shells to consider the dreadful days when an expanding economy eats up fixed income. Meanwhile, you are moving ahead.

Greed. The opposite effect is usually obtained from exerting pressure through appeals to greed. Whereas fear incapacitates, greed agitates. By pressing the greedy, you get their support for almost any motion. Simply point out how your plan will add to their income or possessions and they put aside their fearful hesitation and old hatreds. They follow you in the hope of grabbing another dollar or gaining more power.

Loyalty. Along with its related emotion, duty, loyalty frequently leads people to commit self-sacrificial acts. Pressure the loyal, and you'll get them to participate in jobs they don't like. Like hatred, loyalty can be depended on. Loyal people rarely change. They may resent what they do, even hate it, but their devotion outweighs their other emotional responses.

Such people are ideal subjects for manipulation, provided you don't come up against conflicting loyalties. Suppose you want to ask one of your managers to move to the New York office for the good of the company. His wife is from a small town in Iowa and has always lived in the Midwest. She doesn't want to move out of the area. Here the manager's loyalty to his family conflicts with his loyalty to the company.

You should always know your subject's priority system before making emotional demands. E. M. Forster once said that if he ever had to choose between betraying his country or a friend, he hoped he would have the courage to betray his country. When you find such divided loyalties, you can turn the conflicting one around so that it becomes supportive. With the manager's transfer to the New York office, you point out that his professional advancement would be so beneficial to the provincial wife that she would be happy in a few months. No harm in giving her a chance for growth and change. It isn't an irreversible decision. She may well come to love the city as much as she has loved the country. For her own good she should be asked to experiment with change.

Pity. People are often swayed by pity, a powerful, underexploited emotion. We are a nation of underdog lovers. A sick cat or a beaten football team raises pity in the strongest American spirit. I knew a woman who smoked a particular brand of cigarette because she felt sorry that it was not as popular as others. She said she didn't like the taste, but she wanted to help the company with her business.

Pity is an extremely unstable emotion. It cannot be depended on except for momentary action. After a few days or weeks, the object of pity frequently becomes the object of scorn. Like fear, pity is more useful for protective purposes than for motivating people to action. You can use it to stall some plan or deviate from some projected action, but it is difficult to move people to lengthy, practical change by pity alone.

With pity, as with all emotions, you may not always get the response you expect. You have to be constantly alert to the possibility that some other emotion outweighs the one you are appealing to. Without a thorough knowledge of your subject's emotional patterns, you may get a violent reaction.

Suppose you are trying to pressure someone through greed. Your appeal to this negative emotion activates a positive one— loyalty—and you find an emotionally committed opponent instead of a pressured participant. Whenever emotions are involved, cautious experimentation should precede any attempt at exerting pressure.

Favors

Buttering people up with flattery, personal charm, or a good lunch has become almost an empty ritual in business, more traditional than productive. These business favors, though, are useful pressure devices: they are recognized debts that you can collect as you need them. Someone recommends you for an honor or a promotion. When the time comes, you pay up for the honor by returning the favor. You build up favors the way you build up your savings—so that you can draw on them when times are hard.

A stockbroker once went to see John Pierpont Morgan to borrow money. Morgan said, "I can't lend you the money, but

I'll do something better. I'll walk across the floor of the Exchange with my arm around your shoulder.'' Such favors are free to give, but valuable to receive.

When you dispense favors, do it with style. Don't hand out something grudgingly. Make your slightest gesture a showy one. When pressure forces you to nominate an obnoxious villain for a chairmanship, don't growl while doing it. Make it seem like you've been waiting your whole life for the chance. Before the meeting spend some time on the phone with the vile creature's friends to make sure you have the procedure right. Then present your nomination with the grace of a king bestowing riches on a deserving subject. In this way you submit to inevitable pressures while building up some of your own.

Manipulation is a matter of giving and receiving, and you always have your goodwill to give. Hand it out graciously. Don't let pride make you stiff-necked and ungrateful. Gratitude is an honest payment for favors given. If you look at a generous gesture as if it were a slap in the face, it will become one. You will make your benefactor an enemy unless you show the humble acceptance expected of you.

At some point, of course, favors become bribes. The papers are full of stories about federal officials who take a weekend at the expense of some company only to find—if they are caught—that regulations require that they pay for the trip themselves. Accepting corporate bribes makes you indebted unnecessarily and rarely advances you. It gratifies the ego, thus making you the manipulatee.

Occasionally, though, you will have to play the bribery game because certain people don't think you're important unless you are on someone's bribe list. When your future depends on your rank in the bribery scale, determine the minimum amount necessary for your projected image and accept it. Most of the time all you have to do is indicate that you have been approached; you derive the prestige benefits without the hassle and fear.

The Old-Boy Network

England has built its managerial hierarchy on the buddy system. The right school, the right town, the right friends establish the connections that get you in the Right Company. These personal considerations exert considerable pressure. People are more likely to trust people who are like themselves.

In American businesses too, top managers often have past experiences in common. They may have graduated from the same school or have been members of the same church in suburban Washington 15 years ago. Somewhere along the line, the hiring process finally comes down to personal considerations. And don't be misled by government regulations designed to eliminate discrimination in hiring. Out of a dozen equally qualified candidates, higher-ups will select people they have known or people whose style will perpetuate their own image in the organization.

One successful executive keeps a copy of *Who's Who* by his phone so that when he is talking to someone he can read the biographical sketch and slant his conversation in a personal direction.

The personal slant has been used so often that business golf has become part of the standup comic's routine. Sophisticated managers are now beginning to view golf the way they have viewed bowling—as slightly blue collar. When you try the personal approach for pressure, make sure you are not setting up barriers rather than bridges. Racquetball and skiing, sailing and flying, are now the executives' common bonds. Slopes and strut-stress have replaced greens and irons in the conversation of sharp manipulators. Until you know the personal interests of those above you, be reticent about your own. You can't become part of the set unless you match the standard pattern.

Do not confuse warm professional relationships with friendship. Shared associations at the personal level serve a professional purpose and should not be used to satisfy the ego. Sir

Francis Bacon, who lived at the beginning of the modern business age, spent many years in government. His experience taught him that no relationship is permanent. He once said, "Never say anything to an enemy that would keep him from becoming your friend; never say anything to a friend that he could use against you if he became your enemy."

Bacon's realism has long been thought to be crassly opportunistic. Romantic souls would like to open their hearts to their friends and pour wrath on their enemies. Only when people recognize the limits of the Old-Boy system can they live a rich existence. Even romantic spirits know they can dance on a table with abandon only if they remember where the edges are.

Since friendship is a variable relationship, the pressure you exert on friends can be no stronger than their priority system. If they place themselves, issues, and the organization ahead of friendship, you ought to know that before you call for a vote. When it is time to put the pressure on, you had better know how well your friendship will hold up in the boiler.

Sometimes personal ties prevail. At other times you have to discuss, importune, threaten, or recall unpaid favors before you get friendship up to first place in your subject's priority system. Friendship pressure has to be checked and adjusted each time it is applied.

Sometimes antagonistic personal pressures are easier to handle than friendly ones because they are more visible, reliable, and stable. When you know who your enemies are and why, you know how to exert personal pressure on them for your purpose. Take, for example, rigid authoritarians who must have their own way. They despise you for your receptivity to new ideas, your willingness to change procedures and goals. They'd sooner die than do you a favor.

Knowing their inflexibility, you can depend on it and manipulate it to your advantage. With them you create pressure by resorting to *antifavors*. Since authoritarians will oppose you in everything, you ask for the opposite of what you want. The authoritarian becomes suspicious and shifts to oppose you.

With a slight antagonistic pressure on the antifavor response you manipulate to gain your goal.

You can also pressure authoritarians by publicly praising them for achievements over which they have no control. Give them your gratitude when they don't deserve it, and they will be in your power. A new office procedure is initiated; before they can complain about it, you compliment them on their creative reshaping of a worn-out pattern. Ego and resentment will neutralize each other and incapacitate them from further reasonable opposition to the issue.

Revolutionary types do not respond to the same kind of public pressure. Their self-image is slightly more flexible, but they can still be influenced through the ego. Do them an unexpected favor, and they will be as trapped by ego gratification as the authoritarians.

In personal pressure situations you must not become involved yourself. You should appear enthusiastically involved but remain aloof and apart. You are able to manage pressure by favoritism because emotionalism never clouds your vision. Occasionally, though, you will have to simulate emotions to increase the pressure. With the romantic you can be nostalgic, misty-eyed for the good old days. With the fiery and spirited you can display a pulsating energy. With the cynical you can simulate fear and disappointment. You should always be in charge of the emotion you are manipulating. As a famous politician once said, "I only cry when it will do me some good."

Pulling Strings

A special kind of personal pressure can be exerted by using your relationships with other people to pull strings. This personal influence can be either direct, implied, or illusory.

Direct influence is the pull you clearly have with others along the same power line. An associate tries to threaten your power; you both report to the same superior. You indicate to your equal that you are going to use direct influence with your boss to protect your territory. Once you have made your threat to use direct influence, you must decide if you want to follow through. Like a child caught in a schoolyard squabble, you can always appeal to the teacher. Keep in mind, though, that you do not want to use up your supply of direct influence with too many appeals for aid.

If you do decide to use direct influence, a good approach is to write a letter to your superior. You outline the problem from your point of view and send a copy to your opponent. The formality of such a written appeal is in itself threatening. Your letter, presented in cool, logical prose, will mark you as a purposeful executive who does not fool around when somebody gets in your way. After one letter your reputation for pulling strings will save you from having to use direct influence again to put on the pressure.

For more complex situations you may want to request a conference with the superior and others involved. If you see trouble, you should be the challenger. You choose the conference participants. At the meeting you indicate that your authority has been threatened and that any disorder at your level will result in a challenge to authority all along the line. Most executives realize they have to support the system that supports them.

Always talk honestly with the person holding the string you want to pull. Make your point briefly, and ask for what you want without hedging. Yank your string and let the pressure come out.

Implied influence is the pull you have from knowing influential people. It is less dependent on the power structure. Sometimes all the pressure you need is an allusion to well-placed friends. Name-dropping can elevate you in people's eyes and make them consider your goodwill necessary to their careers.

Of course, name-dropping can easily be countered by dropping heavier names. Once your influence peddler has run out of names, choose one heavy enough to blast the pressure right out of his tank and drop it on the target. You can do it so naturally that the name-dropper won't even be sure he has heard it correctly. You know you have won when he catches his breath, whispers the name to himself, and turns pale.

Illusory influence is the pull you lead opponents to believe you have. You can combine direct and implied influence to set up a dense smokescreen of illusory influence that the unwary subject will never dare to penetrate. Your manipulatee has no way of verifying the authorities you cite because they are so remote as to be in another sphere altogether. Christopher Isherwood tells of an Englishman who lived an almost charmed life in pre-World War II Berlin because some prankster had said that he was a cousin of the English king.

Illusory influence can be fabricated by veiled allusions to clubs you belong to, people you know, places you have been. Sometimes you can even acquire illusory influence by accident. Driving to work once, I turned on an educational radio station and heard a tape of someone speaking at a National Press Club luncheon. I quoted the speaker that afternoon at work and could tell from the hush that came over the group that they thought I had been at the luncheon. As is often the case when an audience is in the grip of an illusion, no one pursued the subject. Of course, I could have easily corrected the illusion and gained myself a strong reputation for honesty. Instead, I left the illusion there, not because I needed it but because I wanted to see if it could survive on its own. It did.

When such windfalls come your way, use them to contribute to your general image. They will help you in the future.

A Powerful Data Base

Some people drop names; others drop information. You can often exert pressure by parading the right knowledge. Letting the people you want to influence know you read the *American Scholar* or the *Yale Review* is sometimes enough to gain your purpose. When a title alone does not silence your enemies, you can increase the pressure with tidbits of impressive information.

Very little research is necessary for putting on data pressure. You can use the same statistics repeatedly in different combinations to demonstrate your profound knowledge of a subject. One executive has trotted out his standard patter on overpopulation at every meeting he has attended for the past ten years. Whatever the event, he rattles off his memorized graph, impressing those who have not heard him before with his keen, well-equipped mind.

In addition to public information, a wealth of material is available in your office memos, letters contradicted by later latters, and all the other paperwork you store in your files. Save all the information you can. You never know when it will be the pressure you are looking for. One unimaginative pressurizer just listens to other people talk at meetings and then hands the information back to them at another time. Nothing is quite so impressive as hearing your own material brought to life again in another person's report.

Private information sometimes creates the most powerful pressure of all. As we saw in the chapter on threat, knowledge of people's private affairs can be a source of control. Just hint that you have insights into someone's private affairs, and the fearful soul will withdraw from the field.

With any kind of data, minimum release is best. No one likes a blabbermouth. You create the illusion of intelligence quickest by keeping your mouth closed. Don't be eager to provide a fact; but if one is divulged, suggest that you've known it all along. It's the same game you play at parties with the "Have you read this book?" routine. A book review is as good as a reading, and sometimes the outline of the book is enough to keep you talking about it for an hour. Probably, nobody else has read it either. Talk only when you have a specific purpose for speaking. You are not in business to gratify your personal needs.

The Money Pouch

One of my friends said to me five years ago, "We don't want legal control. We're going to get hold of the budget and then we'll have things our own way." Within three years he had the budget and, consequently, the control over which programs expanded and which dried up. The ultimate pressure is the power of the purse.

A wise realist told me, "I can buy anyone on this staff for $1,000 more a year than he is making now." Although you may not admire that kind of control, it is certainly real control. Talk money and people run scared. Suppose that someone is suggesting a project that you oppose. You can sink it by showing that it is going to cost more than the present program. If you are the one suggesting a costly program, you can use other kinds of pressure—appeals to legality, friendship, or greed—to counteract the financial arguments that come your way.

Your relationship to budget can take several forms. You have budgets you are personally responsible for, budgets you depend on in whole or in part, and budgets you are working to obtain. In all these cases you can use a variety of pressure tactics—the budget squeeze or the budget reallocation, for example—to get your way. Take the budget squeeze. Where you have budgetary control it is always possible to get your way simply by threatening a budget squeeze. With a combination of prophecy and intimidation you suggest that hard times are coming. Someone is going to feel the pinch. The implication is clear: shape up or the pinch will be in your direction.

Budget reallocation is more specific than the hint at a squeeze. By rearranging budgets in various departments or sections, without any voiced threat whatever you can indicate a clear threat to someone's budding empire. Otto, who was ambitiously pushing toward a vice-presidency through his general services section, became a threat to the present vice-president, Mr. M. Seeing the situation, M recommended that certain service budgets be turned over to personnel and consolidated in that section. After several such gradual reallocations, it became clear to Otto that his power was being curtailed rather than increased. The threat was so real to him that he moved to another company rather than fight the reallocation pattern that had been set up against his advancement.

Budget should never be underestimated. It is the primary type of pressure upon which most of us depend. A constant awareness of your relationship to budget may determine how free you are to exert other kinds of pressure to balance out pressures from the money pouch.

High-Pressure Hal

In ten years Hal has moved from salesman to executive vice-president. He talked to me at length about how he used pressure for manipulation.

JONES: You've been telling me about some of the ways you've used pressure. What do you think is the most effective way?

HAL: If I were advising others about pressure, the first thing I'd tell them to do is to observe. You can learn a lot about somebody by watching. You waste a lot of good pressure if you exert the wrong kind. You have to know the type of pressure a person is suceptible to.

JONES: What do you mean?

HAL: Well, when I first started working I watched a man who seemed impervious to any argument or influence. He paid no attention to what other people wore, so I knew he didn't care about what others thought of him. He didn't even seem to care about money.

During my first two years with the company, I watched that man resist all kinds of pressure. I liked him, but I got to wondering if I could find his weak spot. I knew he was a big family man. That and his church were the center of his life. He was quiet about it, but he taught Sunday school. That's how I got on to the right pressure. Once I said quietly to him, "What those people are doing is really *immoral,* don't you think?" After that, we were allies. When anybody pulled a shrewd trick, I'd look at this guy with amazement and play the moralist.

JONES: You don't think it's dishonest to dissemble like that?

HAL: Hell, no! I'm not even sure it's dissembling. I extract from my personality the part that fits somebody else's and put on the pressure. When you're trying to tighten a bolt, you look at your wrenches to find out which fits best, don't you? You'd be a fool to use a big one on a little bolt. When I'm trying to put on the pressure, I look in my pressure kit and take out what fits best.

JONES: If you were going to advise people on how to resist pressure, what would you say?

HAL: First of all, I'd tell them not to be rigid. I've pulled some of my best stunts by applying pressure to the most rigid part of somebody's personality. A lot of pressures don't hurt if you bend under them. It's when you get your back up and resist that you crack. When the pressure is on, as with the moralist Sunday-school teacher, you have to decide whether you want to be manipulated. You've got two choices: to continue bending or to stand firm.

I won't say that I'm invulnerable to pressure. I suppose financial pressure is the one that talks loudest to me; but there are some things I won't do even for money. Still, when somebody talks to me about budget, I think long and hard. Sometimes you can let the pressure slip by you so that you accomplish what you want anyway. Once somebody came at me with the threat of a budget cut in my department. All I had to do was to find another department that could stand the cut better than mine. I brought other pressures to bear—personal relationships, statistics. I tried to pile up as many other pressures as possible, and I finally built up enough to resist the pressure coming down on me.

That is what you've got to do, I guess, although I've never thought about it in just this way before. It's a matter of forces. Equal forces counteract each other; superior force prevails and moves things. Pressure is just a kind of force.

JONES: I guess so. It's probably as permanent a part of our lives as gravitational pull.

HAL: Pull is what I've got now. I can talk to you like this because if you told everybody in this building what I've said, I could set up a pressure system by tomorrow that would have them throwing rocks at you.

JONES: You're right, but I won't be here tomorrow. One kind of pressure that we haven't even talked about is the pressure of time. I've got to be going. Thanks for talking with me.

10

SCHEMES

Finding the Right Mix

MANAGERS are somewhat hesitant to call scheming by its right name. Terms such as "long-range planning," "predictive thinking," "contingency considerations," and "restructuring" obscure the real purpose of this manipulative technique: getting what you want as cheaply as you can. Admit your actual purpose, and you are ahead of those who refuse to use the real term for the real thing. By deluding themselves as to their intention, they becloud their creative process.

A scheme is a complex manipulative procedure that combines several techniques we have already studied. Basically, it consists of (1) establishing a purpose, (2) selecting specific manipulative devices that will achieve it, and (3) floating the project delicately, with a watchful eye on the participants. The process is the same whether you are engaged in a simple plan for personal advancement or a corporate effort to control the nation's gas supply.

Here is a scheme at its simplest level. Jeb wants to catch a bus that leaves his office corner at 4:55 every day. He is supposed to work until 5:00. To start with, he has to decide if his purpose is achievable. He decides that by leaving the office seven minutes early he can make it to that bus.

Schemers who stop here may run out to catch the bus only

to encounter the boss at the same stop. They have failed to consider a power structure that permits higher executives to leave early. To pursue a scheme without considering all the possibilities leads to frustration and a sometimes costly victory. Creative schemers know that bosses catch early buses. Then they examine their real purpose. It is not to catch one particular bus but to get home as soon as possible.

Revising his scheme, Jeb realizes that another bus leaves a block away at 4:57. On that corner he will not be seen by people in his building. Sheltered from the local power center, he leaves nothing to chance. He innocently asks around the office to find out how people get home after work. He even establishes an alibi for his last few minutes by setting his digital desk clock a few minutes fast. Then he leaves by the rear exit and takes an express that gets him home five minutes earlier than the one he could have made by running out the front door.

Flexibility and constant reexamination of purpose are essential in complex schemes. Frequently, the purpose as originally stated is not the actual purpose. Wise manipulators do not close their minds to the need for change. As they uncover obstacles to their schemes or new possibilities, they remain optimistic, because they know that success can be obtained in innumerable ways. It is simply a matter of finding the best solution.

Successful scheming depends on the absolute conviction that you can achieve your purpose. To that extent, almost all constructive human effort comes under the general heading of scheming. You want a good job, so you get a good education that is suited to market needs, and your scheme—life plan, if you prefer—works. Failure to assess market needs carefully can thwart your scheme. Latest reports indicate that by 1990 only one in five Ph.D.s will be able to find university employment. If you majored in Old Irish at Harvard you may find that only two schools in the country have positions for you. You did not pay out your scheme with a realistic survey of opportunities.

Once your purpose has been established, the most creative and difficult part of scheming lies ahead of you. You have to determine manipulative devices that will get you where you want to go. Out of the numerous manipulative skills you have already acquired, you extract the simplest and most appropriate ones for your particular situation. Again, suppose you are trying to develop a job-training plan for your future. If you approach the problem with one job in mind, your rigidity will make you vulnerable to failure; if you set a general area and prepare for several job possibilities, you do not limit yourself.

In both planning and implementation you must retain *scheme diversity.* You wander through a maze of dead ends and wonder if your scheme will work. If you have worked out only a single route to the center, it probably won't. If, on the other hand, you have five different possibilities open at all times, you can run in another direction without wasting time and effort. As one friend expressed his philosophy of scheming: "The rat with only one hole to run to doesn't last very long."

Power Flow

Whether you call it a plan, a project, a con job, or a scheme, you have to know where the power is flowing. As many schemes fail because of self-doubt as because of overconfidence. One manager, who had been shuffled into a dead-end position, said, "If I had known how stupid and powerless the people I was competing with were, I'd have been president of the company by now." This executive had never dared to scheme because he lacked a realistic understanding of his relationship to the power flow around him. Whatever your position, you are within reach of some power source. It changes hands from time to time, but you need to know where it is. Is it concentrated in one person? Or, as more often happens, is it distributed among many?

A good way to locate the power source is by volunteering your efforts. As you work for others at thankless tasks, you will hear certain names mentioned over and over. Some of these people will have *positional power*, derived from their place in the corporate heirarchy. Others will have *functional power*, derived from their day-to-day responsibilities.

The owner of a company has positional power because of his investment. The manager of the company has functional power because he does the hiring and implements policy. If the manager decides not to maintain the ventilator system that the law and the owner have required to be installed, functional power gains the advantage as long as the neglected system goes unnoticed.

The owner's major concern is profit; the manager has the added concern of daily operation. The manager's practical understanding of line action gives him an advantage over the more remote owner. The owner, therefore, is likely to defer to the manager's wisdom. If the owner ceases to trust the manager's judgment, he can assert his positional power and replace the manager. The manager's replacement then steps in and reactivates the functional power flow.

The interplay between these two types of power creates a strong undertow. Don't get caught in it. A clear understanding of positional and functional power is essential to the success of your well-laid schemes. The people with functional power are the ones closest to daily decisions. You gain little advantage by lunching with the company president if your position is being phased out by your immediate superior.

One manager, who prided himself on having a friend on the governing board, ran to his friend when he got into trouble with his unit manager. "I can't do anything about that," the board member said. "I'd look foolish meddling in trivial affairs." Smart schemers may appeal to positional power once in a while, but they know that functional power is the energy source to tap.

People in positional power are often receptive to adulation. They like to see a snappy salute from their second lieutenants. Many of these lieutenants are inflating their own egos through the relationship. Let them enjoy their superior's company while you scheme at ground level to accomplish what you want.

Sometimes the success of a scheme depends on how much power the schemer can produce. Morris wanted to award a contract to a particular company. He knew that if he sent his recommendation through regular channels it would take three months. The company needed the business right away. Morris found that the procedure for awarding contracts had varied widely over the past three years. He checked and found that no specific regulation covered the kind of request he was going to make. Without sending his request through purchasing, he handled the contract out of his own budget. When it was challenged, the people with functional power said, "It's done. There's nothing specifically illegal about it. Just don't do it again."

Schemes like Morris's work only once. Other schemes become precedents for future actions. A department was trying to hire a research scientist who was being sought by two other companies. Knowing how important electron microscopes were for this man's research, the head of the department borrowed two from a neighboring division and set them up in the lab the man would use if he took the job. The scientist accepted the offer.

When he arrived on the job, the scientist asked where the microscopes were. "They were being stored here temporarily," the scheming department chief said. "We can't afford electron microscopes." Since that time, others in the plant have developed the practice of "storing" equipment whenever attractive job candidates visit their labs.

Schemes need not be harmful to future relationships. Scheming has become so prevalent that most people no longer hold grudges against a schemer. The exploits of creative schemers are retold as if they were the achievements of culture heroes. I have heard of a football coach who imports his players from West Virginia coal-mining towns and keeps them so poor that they can't leave. Then there's the newspaper editor who flies his staff into his remote area and pays them so little that they work for years trying to get the money to get out of town.

Preparing the Mixture

Schemes should suit the personality of the schemer. There are three major kinds of schemes: spontaneous, problem-solving, and collusive. The first two types work well for individualists and loners. The third is better suited to team players.

The *spontaneous scheme* is a favorite of disorganized people whose impatience keeps them from planning intricate, long-range intrigue. Spontaneous schemes are the manipulator's equivalent of stealing bases. A sharp eye and fast footwork will get you around the bases as quickly as steady batting.

The spontaneous schemer always has an eye out for a scheme. Sitting at lunch, for example, he overhears a secretary comment that she has just posted an application form for a good-service award on the bulletin board. The schemer goes to the bulletin board and rearranges it so that the notice is hidden under older ones. Then he nominates a friend for the award. Since no one else is nominated, the friend wins the free trip for two to Hawaii. He doesn't take his wife. He takes the schemer who nominated him.

Spontaneous scheming requires a daredevil mentality. Truly sporting spirits use it throughout their careers. With a delicate sensitivity to unstable situations—a new position opening up, a marriage on the rocks, an old friendship breaking down—they use spontaneous scheming to wrest success out of momentary chaos.

Cultivating an eye for unstable moments is essential to spontaneous scheming. Symptoms of unrest usually let you know when a daredevil steal is safe. You have to trust your instinctive responses to situations. Most mornings you go to work expecting the normal routine; one day you get to work and feel a particular dread, an uneasiness that you can't describe. It is not physical as much as psychological. Unless you have had a particularly bad night, you may have stumbled on an opportunity for spontaneous scheming. Check your instinct by talking to several others in the office. Do they too seem glum today? Do they wonder why things are not going right? If the mood is widespread, seek out the cause.

The cause may be nothing more than a low day for Dow Jones, a big contract that fell through, or a key secretary who is away for the week. For most people these events are inconsequential; for the schemer they lay bare opportunities that are usually heavily clothed in protective garments. Financial setbacks, professional insecurity, the inability to find things in the files—any number of irritations can be turned into advantages by the spontaneous schemer.

C.T. discovered that the office routine had been disturbed because the staff was shorthanded. He had been trying to get approval on a project that was shelved several years ago. In a moment of spontaneous inspiration he decided that now was the time to talk to the boss about approval.

With C.T.'s luck as a spontaneous schemer, no one knew where the files on the project were. Totally dependent on C.T.'s account of the history of the project, the boss gave tentative approval for reactivating it. By the time the secretary came back, the boss had moved on to other concerns. C.T. simply gave her a copy of the office memo endorsing the project; she put it in the file and C.T. proceeded with his job. The boss had been so distracted without adequate support staff that he didn't even remember giving his approval until it was time for the annual report. By then the project was well on the way to completion.

More methodical manipulators use the *problem-solving scheme.* Like the bus-stop manipulator, they set themselves a goal and devise a carefully thought-out plan to achieve it. These methodical types work best through committee manipulation and policy restatement. Their associates usually say, "No doubt who's going to be in control now. And Joe deserves it. He's been scheming for it for years."

The danger with this kind of scheming is that it takes so much time and energy. Preoccupation with problem-solving schemes makes the world a rocky brook that you have to cross without getting your feet wet. It is sometimes more fun to try a big jump, taking a chance on falling in.

Still, if you want to become a first-rate schemer, you should try your hand at problem solving. It is excellent training in rational thinking, an ability necessary for cool-headed manipulators of all breeds. As you gain the control needed to set your goal and make arrangements for getting there, people will come to think of you as a natural leader with purpose and drive.

The stumbling block for most problem solvers is lack of imagination. If you can combine cool rationality with a dash of spontaneous scheming, you will come up with an individualized package that gets you what you want.

Lola wanted a larger salary, but she didn't want to move to a new position to get it. She was not in line for a raise, but she decided to scheme for it anyway. She knew that her boss hated one manager with a burning contempt. She decided that the manager could help her get the raise. She went to him to talk about transferring to his department. His hatred for Lola's boss made him enjoy the thought of stealing her away at an awkward time.

When her boss found out what she was doing—by planned accident he discovered it—he called Lola in and told her she could not leave. He met her salary demands and felt he had put something over on his enemy. Actually, the enemy was just as happy to have the boss spending money for an early raise, which always causes bad feelings in a department.

At least half of all successful schemes are developed by manipulators who band others together for a *collusive scheme.* Colluding schemers combine the best characteristics of the other two types: the sensitivity and alertness of spontaneous schemers and the rational ability of problem solvers. In addition, they have the help of a like-minded community of schemers who provide checks against things they might overlook. These partners in crime also become scouts for new schemes.

The danger with collusive scheming is betrayal by a member of the group. But if you are willing to take the risk, collusion will advance you most quickly. Ken saw that a hardworking division chief was rapidly getting ahead of him in budget appropriations. He went to talk to two friends, not to plan a scheme but to discuss the situation. Together they decided that slander would solve their problem.

Since the offending manager's reputation was spotless, they began a smear campaign on his department. One by one they pointed out to the board members that the division was archaic and outmoded. Before long, the board agreed to curtail the hardworking manager's budget and reallocate it to a more "useful" department.

Collusive scheming is a normal defense tactic in organizations of all sizes. Once you select your group, you must determine your purpose and the manipulative techniques necessary to achieve it. Since group selection is the key to successful collusion, the rest of the chapter is devoted to ways of developing and maintaining adequate groups to draw on when you prepare collusive schemes.

Sneer Groups

Sneer groups are composed of people loosely joined together by common prejudices and training. They are frequently so intangible as not to be recognized either by members or outsiders, but they exist in every organization. You can spot them simply by identifying the people who scorn the same things—attitudes, objects, and other people.

These groups develop naturally in organizations because of the diversity of opinions and backgrounds and may cause polarization that continues for years. Wise manipulators identify the various sneer groups in an organization and use them for collusive scheming. They do not ally themselves with any group until they have determined which way the power is flowing. Even then, they keep an opening into all factions so they can use sneer groups without being absorbed by them.

When sneer groups are not highly elitist, you can move into several of them, extract their alert, powerful members, and reorganize them into a new group that shares your own sneer concept. You become the natural leader. If you are planning an unusually grand scheme, you will need to develop such a specialized faction to achieve your purpose.

At the national level sneer groups are more clearly organized into various associations, unions, and clubs. Whether this group is a national advisory board or a local social committee, an alert manipulator spots a group that has power through its sneer pattern and then joins in the sneering. One clear example of the way struggles for power develop between rival sneer groups is the area of federally funded medical research. Government bureaucrats, who sneer at the narrow academic background of scientists, are anxious to exert fiscal control over allocations. Academic scientists, on the other hand, equally anxious to control the direction of the flow of federal money, sneer at the nonspecialists who intrude on their territory.

In every area where federal funds are being allocated, sneer groups develop so that they can exert their pressure to gain money or political power. Rumor has it that when a poetry professor was given a year off with federal funds, the sneer group dominant in that area realized that the only worthy replacement on campus was the federal administrator who had awarded the professor the grant. A good schemer is always alert to such small-circle exchanges. Sneer groups sometimes cooperate, sometimes squabble. You can take advantage of either situation if you add your sneers to those of the ruling clique.

Most sneer groups are too large to be used effectively for collusive schemes. Clever schemers take advantage of the large base of support they provide and select reliable members for a special scheme. Sneer groups are internally divisive. Their dominant mood is negative. For the most part, members

sneer at each other as well as at outsiders. They have little sense of loyalty or ethics. They are composed largely of people who are disappointed with their own achievements. By belittling others, they hope to bolster their own sagging egos.

You will be manipulated by sneer groups if you listen seriously to their constant harangues against workers, managers, secretarial staff, phone service, cafeteria food, and everything else that their contempt has brought to their attention. Participation in these groups can contaminate your view of the universe. You must become immune to their biliousness if you want to advance your scheming.

In most sneer groups those who complain loudest are least likely to come through when they are needed. Jay came to hospital management straight out of college. The director of the hospital was an M.D. specializing in dermatology. Several surgeons and budget officers took Jay to lunch and pointed out that dermatology was practiced only by halfwits. It was just a question of time until some intelligent, practical member of their group replaced the director, whose financial incompetence was only slightly inferior to his professional incompetence.

Jay advanced in the hospital, continuing to listen in awe to the sneerers. When Jay was asked to evaluate his work with the director, he thought this was the chance he had been waiting for to replace the director with someone from his own sneer group. The director had always been cold and distant, and Jay had no respect for him.

Jay talked to his luncheon cronies, who encouraged him to speak up in front of the governing board about the director's incompetence. Jay aired his grievances, pointing out that others were behind him in his evaluation. "Strange," the chairman of the board said, "we've heard no complaint from anyone else. Are you sure of widespread discontent?"

Jay said he would get statements from others to back up his position. Needless to say, no statements were forthcoming. His sneer group had been sneering privately to board members

about Jay's inexperience and incompetence. The upshot of the investigation was that Jay was fired and the surgeons and fiscal managers continued their harmless sneering—harmless to them, but not to anyone who took it seriously.

Sneering has to be heard on the symbolic level. It reveals much more about the sneerers than about the scorned. Once you know the biases and weaknesses of the sneerers, you can manipulate the members of the group by appealing to their fears and secret shames. But you must never look for anything except negative support from most members of a sneer group.

Coteries

The positive version of a sneer group is a coterie. Its members will usually give you active support because they are motivated by deep group loyalties. The world of business advances much more rapidly from backscratching than from backstabbing.

When you enter a managerial position, you will want to learn the local, regional, and national pressure groups and their leaders. Then find out what it takes to become "one of them" and meet those requirements. The entrance fee is never too high if you get into the group with power. As we have seen, colluding schemes depend on belonging to the right support group.

Even though it may seem impossible to meet the requirements of certain coteries—the Ivy Leaguers, the Cal Tech–MIT alliance, the Catholics, the Mormons, the feminists—you should not give up hope. These groups are always willing to accept equivalency diplomas from eager learners. If you ape their basic prejudices and attitudes on crucial issues, they will be glad to let you join their clique.

If you enter a group by the equivalency-diploma method, you may feel that you have surrendered your personal integrity. Don't look at it from that romantic, unrealistic point of view. You have simply conned your way in. Your self-image should still be intact. Compromise for the purpose of manipulation does not tarnish the halo of your true spirit.

The entrance exam is only your first requirement. You will be asked to contribute regularly to the clique's continued supremacy. When you give, give as the Pharisees did. Sound the trumpets and turn on the spotlights. You want to get credit for every success you bring to the group. If someone in your coterie is given an award or a promotion, let everyone know that you were instrumental in getting the nomination. If you pull in a government contract, spread the word around.

When you have something of your own to contribute, consult several members of your group about the best way of awarding the favor. Make sure you bestow it on someone in a collaborating group so that the debt of gratitude will quickly be repaid.

Within the clique-riddled corporate structure the individual is helpless. Since you have to commit yourself to some coterie, you may as well choose the one with the most efficient alliances. Subjective considerations such as friendship and personal interests should not enter into the decision. You ally yourself with the group that has the best connections.

Coteries are held together by many different ties. All these bonds are useful to petition and dangerous to antagonize. The following list is a representative sampling, to which you can add your own discoveries.

THE SCHOOL   From grade school on, you can see the school bond at work. Students who went to the same elementary school stick together when they get to high school. Those from the same high school feel an affinity when they meet again in college. This same-school tie carries over into your career. The common experiences of your high school or college days form the basis for a coterie of people of your own kind. Even if you were not particularly friendly with former schoolmates, the fact that you had the same teachers, ate at the same restaurants, or dated some of the same people brings you together on a positive note.

How you exploit that experience is up to you. Some coteries

are extremely active with regular alumni luncheons, membership rolls, and dues. Others are fairly low key. If you are
interested in organizing a coterie, either out of interest or for
manipulative purposes, the old school tie is a strong rope to
hang on to.

TRAINING AND WORK EXPERIENCE   Similar training and work
experience are strong bonds for creating coteries. A scientist
who has worked at Argonne National Laboratories or the
Communicable Disease Center in Atlanta is drawn to others
who can talk about the same labs, the same problems. People
acquire the unstated prejudices and attitudes of the organizations they work for. These attitudes form the basis for coteries
when people gather together again in other organizations.

The training bond is particularly strong when people are
approximately the same age. They work well together because
they are likely to agree in both philosophy and procedure. This
professional trust carries over into private relationships.

Professional training sometimes outweighs school ties in
shaping coteries. A chemical engineer from one school works
well with a chemical engineer from another; yet he is apt to be
suspicious of people trained in environmental engineering or
other fields, even if they are former schoolmates. Experiences
other than professional training can also be a bond. Chemists
who were in the Navy may side with one another against chemists who graduated from the same college. There is no hard-
and-fast rule for priorities in coteries, but earlier and more
prolonged ties seem to dominate.

SEX, AGE, AND GEOGRAPHY Sex, age, and regional similarities provide a natural nucleus for coteries. Women are likely to
band together against men, young against old, Easterners
against Midwesterners. Although our society gives superficial
approval to the mingling of types, separatism prevails in many
organizations. The advantage of regional, sex, and age bonds
is their universality. Everyone is from somewhere; even if you

grew up in a small town you are likely to be working with someone from your local area or home state. And almost every work group includes members of both sexes; if you are in a totally male or female environment, you will have to find some other basis for your coterie.

I have seen young Turk coteries develop regularly. Wheeling free in their inexperienced idealism, they join to overthrow the ruling elders. If you are practical enough to be both young and wise, you can make use of this natural formation to advance your purposes. I have known young people who talk high revolution do a turnaround when they get promoted: they bow and scrape to the ruling elders while finking on their former colleagues. Ties of sex, age, and locale are not sacred where manipulation is concerned, so scheme with an eye to your back at all times.

PROFESSIONAL SOCIETIES   Professional societies are not nearly as important for schemers as other coteries, but they can become useful lobby groups if you take over. With the current popularity of these groups, you can even start your own society. People are so anxious to advance that by developing a journal you can immediately become the leader of a coterie with national visibility.

Although others may sneer at your newness, they will be grateful if you publish their papers in your quarterly or invite them to speak at your national convention—even if only 15 charter members attend. Established professional societies are sometimes encrusted with barnacles, but you can always chip away a few or start a second layer.

The advantage of professional societies is their aura of distinction. For your own self-image it is a good idea to compete for a position as leader of a seminar or secretariat. Professional coteries give you dignity and encouragement. As with all groups, though, remember that the dignity and prestige are only as good as your professional position. Don't be deceived into believing that the fame you derive from coteries is lasting or of great tangible value except as a manipulative device. Trade on the Manager of the Year award as quickly as you can, because someone else will be receiving it next year.

Warring Factions

If there are three members in an organization, two of them will be ganging up on the third. Good schemers do not deplore this antagonism; they use it to their advantage. Warring factions are sneer groups or coteries in conflict. To manipulate them, you must first distinguish between their stated cause of difference and the actual cause. The factionalism, which has usually existed over a long period of time, has become ritualized. Whatever people in one group do, the opposing group is likely to criticize.

The factions probably originated because of professional jealousies and conflicting professional attitudes. These have now been padded with layers of resentment and petty malice. When you hear stories of business stupidity, unethical actions, and benighted incompetence, look at the personalities involved to find the real truth under the accusations. The leaders are probably trying to use the factions for their own advancement.

Sometimes a faction may be unaware that its real purpose is to stir up trouble. It may be passively, even scornfully, enduring the strife while pursuing other matters. If so, you can step in and take active control. With other factions, you can divide and conquer. If two groups have equally aggressive leaders, you can play them against each other.

Factions are in conflict either because it is their natural state or because you or someone else has activated them. Once set in motion, factions have no morality or braking power. They will self-destruct before they will draw back. Trying to control such a group is like trying to stop a runaway locomotive by dragging your feet on the ground. Warring factions are usually on a collision course.

When factions battle, the best approach is to lie low and

direct the action from as far away as possible. You can't stop the war, but you can shift the action to a different front. If, for example, the bombs are dropping too close to your front door, you can point out the real target, which is certainly not you, and hope that the fire will go over your head.

In planning collusion, you will have to work with the factional patterns that exist, unless you are willing to devote a great deal of time to rearranging them. That is almost like trying to chair a Paris peace conference. It is much more economical to point the factions at each other and let them blow themselves up. Then you can crawl out from the wreckage and build a coterie that is directed toward achieving goals that will advance your cause.

Ted, Sylvia, and Other Schemers

The following discussion took place in the cafeteria of a Washington agency where scheming was outwardly scorned but secretly admired. The divergent attitudes of the managers present indicate how necessary group communication is. The participants around the table were Ted, a 35-year-old chemist; Sylvia, a 50-year-old personnel manager; Pete, a 28-year-old budget officer; Sid, a 40-year-old corporate lawyer; and Jones, a visitor.

JONES: You people have such different jobs that I don't suppose you have much in common to talk about.

SID: In government bureaucracies you can always talk about trying to beat the old system. Right, Sylvia?

SYLVIA: Sid is kidding me because he thinks I hear about all the schemes from people who come in to get transfers. Well, I do have quite a collection of sad tales.

One management specialist told me that he was being chewed out by another manager in his section. Looking up at his clock, he suddenly thought in a moment of inspiration that it would be good if he could give the man a reputation for chronic lateness. So every time he had a

chance he'd set the guy's clock back. His victim was late
to three meetings in a row. The poor dope got a new clock,
but the schemer kept on changing the time. Eventually the
victim got in trouble with his boss. The schemer profited
from the split.

PETE: How did you hear that story?

SYLVIA: The schemer told me about it when he came to ask
for a transfer. He made the mistake of bragging about the
trick, and the others in the office were so antagonistic that
he couldn't stand it.

TED: The first law of scheming is "Keep your mouth shut."

SID: That's where the big crooks have it over the little ones.
The crooks we work with don't go out and get drunk,
bragging about the money they just stole.

TED: What do you mean, big crooks? We work with big
grants, and we negotiate with each other about how to
award them. We don't do anything dishonest.

SID: I was using the word "crook" as a complimentary term.
The people I work with don't brag about their successful
schemes, but a sizable mythology has developed around
heroes who have pulled off something big in the way of
"negotiations."

PETE: You guys are shocking me. I thought you advanced
grade by grade on the basis of merit.

SID: Oh, to be young again! We don't mean to laugh at you,
Pete, but when you say things like that you should try to
get an ironic edge to your voice. You sounded as if you
meant it.

SYLVIA: I'm afraid you advance by scheming and getting in
with the strong crowd. I sometimes wonder if even the
pure scientists don't get ahead because they're politically
astute enough to join the right societies and the right research teams.

TED: Of course, Sylvia. I can't think of any place that right
connections are more important than in chemistry. You
start out at the right school, doing research in a lab with

some "big names" in it. They put you in touch with others who will let you do their dirty work for them. Then, when you've published with a big name long enough, you become a big name yourself. I don't think anybody gets anywhere alone. They call it "the scholarly community."

SYLVIA: It's the same for managers. You don't exist except in a circle. Around here you've got to learn the committee system. That's the way the place runs.

SID: And what you brag about is not your research or your writing but what governing board or council you have been appointed to for the year.

TED: We shouldn't be surprised that connections make the difference. Jesus chose a committee of 12 to help him get started, and they were pretty representative of the kinds of people he wanted to influence.

SYLVIA: Pretty good example. Nobody does anything alone.

SID: We'll all agree that it is necessary to be in the right circle professionally. But how would you advise people to get in? And, after they're in, what would you advise them to do to keep from being swallowed by the corporate body?

SYLVIA: Getting in with the right crowd professionally is like running in on jumprope. Keep your eyes open, get your feet ready, and make your move when you think the time is right.

PETE: And if the rope hits you in the face?

SYLVIA: You go to the end of the line and wait for another chance to run in.

SID: The circles are easiest to enter in the new fields. I know an engineer—a university dean—who got into computers near the beginning. He had one installed at his university and made the right connections with the Big Company. In the last five years he has made over half a million as a consultant for businesses that want to install similar systems. The company recommends him, and he decides that the plant can't do better than to go with the Big Company. Others might do the job cheaper, but who knows whether they'll be around to service next year? The Big Company will last.

SYLVIA: And so will the dean's extra income. That game of holding a university administrative position while serving as consultant is a valuable scheme. If you can get two rewarding groups circling, you're in the money. The university thinks the administrator is more valuable because of his external contacts; the external contacts think the university position gives the fellow status.

SID: And it does. That's what you can't argue with. The way the system works, the dean is doing right to milk it. Who's to say his motives aren't pure?

PETE: You don't think he should be doing something for education or industry rather than for himself?

SYLVIA: Don't be unrealistic, Pete. Get your circles working for you. And don't feel guilty. Look at it this way. If you weren't making the rakeoff, someone else would be, someone far less qualified and probably greedier than you. You're doing the system a favor by hanging in there yourself instead of letting some unscrupulous manager get hold.

JONES: You're lucky, Pete, to be learning from these veterans. Maybe they'll let you play fall guy for their next scheme.

11

PREJUDICE

Appealing to the Worst

PREJUDICE is the sleeping giant in everyone. It springs up unexpectedly to chase Jack down the beanstalk and then falls asleep again. If you are the Jack being chased, you need a thorough knowledge of the giant's sleeping habits. Unless you can anticipate and control this seemingly unreasonable response, the irrational and erratic behavior of prejudiced people will destroy your most carefully planned manipulations.

Prejudice is not an Archie Bunker response, remote from the world of executive management. It is a source of unexpected behavior in all of us. Lionel was a gentle, pleasant man with whom I occasionally drank coffee. I would have sworn he had no ill will toward anyone. Then he began having trouble at one of his weekly committee meetings. He dreaded attending it, grew irritable, and lashed out at other members. He could not sleep the night after the meeting. After a while, his secretary of many years requested a transfer to another department; his wife and children commented on his personality change—to each other, not to him.

He rarely talked about the committee, but one day at coffee he began complaining to me of the problems that were ruining his life. I laughingly said, "I don't mean to be personal, but you haven't gone impotent, have you?"

"Quite the opposite," he said bitterly. "I'm screwing more and enjoying it less. But what does that have to do with my personality? Are you a Freudian or something?"

"No, but I noticed that everything you complain about has to do with women. You have trouble with your secretary; you quarrel with your wife. Even your mother has come in for a violent kick or two lately. I figured your trouble was sexual."

Lionel's eyes widened in a slightly glazed stare; he turned red. "It's that damned committee," he said. "You know what they've done. They've made me secretary—and there are three women on it! Being secretary is a woman's job."

Lionel's trouble had begun when the chairman of the committee asked him to take notes at the meetings. When he had to prepare the minutes with his secretary, he took his resentment out on her. When he presented the minutes at the next meeting, the shame of doing "women's work" made him irritable. If the committee had been composed entirely of men, Lionel would not have been ashamed of taking the minutes. With three women present, he felt that he had been debased and his masculinity insulted.

Lionel's affliction follows the standard prejudice pattern. When we stereotype jobs and people, we lose touch with reality and increase our frustration. Lionel had always assumed that prejudice was destructive only to its recipients, those who were excluded from the happy majority. He saw now that he had suffered a great deal more than the victims of his unconscious antifeminism.

Until the committee stuck Lionel with "a woman's job," he had always had especially good working relationships with women. As we talked at coffee, it became clear to him that these pleasant conditions had existed because he had regarded them as his inferiors. They did not threaten him with competition the way males did.

It would be falsifying the story to say that Lionel had a moment of truth in the coffee shop and was washed clean of his sexist bias. But he did begin to understand that his resentment over being made secretary was spoiling previously satisfactory relationships at home and at work.

A few weeks later Lionel told me, "I'm surprised to find that once I located the cause of my irritation I began to feel better about it. I still think the chairman insulted me by giving me that job, but now I focus my hatred on the chairman, not the women."

"Do you think the chairman intentionally tried to insult you when he gave you the job of taking notes?" I asked him.

The question was another moment of truth for Lionel. It had never occurred to him that everyone did not share his view of the inferior status of women in business. If the chairman saw everyone on the committee as equals, independent of sexual differences—in other words, if he saw them as co-workers with similar talents and responsibilities—he might have been paying Lionel a compliment when he asked him to take accurate, intelligent notes of the committee proceedings.

Lionel's experience is typical of the way prejudice works in business. Until you learn to recognize the largely unconscious biases in yourself and others, you will not be in control of your actions. That lack of self-control handicaps you when you try to control others. Knowledge of your biases extends your power so that you know when to leave prejudice sleeping and when to arouse it for manipulative purposes.

As with Lionel, once you become aware of prejudice, you can control it and use it to your advantage. The Five-Point Prejudice Guide outlined below will help you identify the causes and manifestations of prejudice. Manipulators do not scruple to use this information because they are always sure that their manipulations are more worthy than the leading competitor's. Start with this guide and learn how to appeal to the worst, in yourself and others.

The Five-Point Prejudice Guide

Whether the prejudice is yours or someone else's the process for discovering it is the same. Keep the five key points in mind while you're seeking out prejudices and make mental notes about what you see. You will find the prejudice harvest a bountiful one.

DOG KICKING   You know the story about the man who comes home from work and yells at his wife. She slaps the child, who kicks the dog. The angry dog bites the man who yelled at his wife. This is the classic example of transferred aggression. Unable to respond directly to the source of irritation, people seek out weaker ones they can hurt safely.

The first place to spot prejudice is at the dog-kicking stage. It is the most immediate and widespread manifestation of prejudice and can usually be traced back to its origins. If you are the dog being kicked, it is difficult to be dispassionate about it. Still, you are wiser to look behind the kick to discover its real cause. Then, in your relationship with the prejudiced kicker, you can demonstrate the real source of irritation and divert the kick to the backside of some other helpless cur.

THE INSECURITY BLANKET   Prejudice is a loincloth for naked fear. When you see someone kicking the dog, take a reading of when it occurs. It usually happens shortly after someone's security has been threatened. For those in the advanced stages of prejudice, fear and insecurity have become chronic. They kick the dog almost constantly. Still, as with Lionel's attitude toward women, if you see enough examples of the kicking you will be able to uncover the basic source of insecurity.

Insecurity is most often related to some threat to a person's financial condition. Since women were usually paid less than men, Lionel unconsciously feared that to be treated like one was a threat to his earning ability.

Sometimes the educational and the financial intermingle to weave the insecurity blanket. One department was composed of three Ph.D.s, each earning over $30,000 a year; ten managers, who had come up through the ranks, each making $18,000; and about twenty staff members, each making around $11,000.

The managers, who were the controlling majority in the department, resented the Ph.D.s' educational and financial superiority and tried in little ways to make life difficult for them. The Ph.D.s, who were functionally dependent on the managers, transferred their resentment to the staff workers. Unable to kick the managers, whom they really resented, they turned on the staff, whom they ridiculed for ignorance and incompetence. Nasty incidents multiplied and resulted in periodic purges of the staff at the insistence of the Ph.D.s.

As you can see from this example, prejudice is often contagious. The resentment of the managers spread to two other levels as well. When I was called in to analyze the situation, I thought I had stepped into a pit of hissing snakes. All three groups were shaking their rattles at one another in constant warning to stay clear.

I saw the prejudices that had resulted from economic and educational insecurity. The three Ph.D.s, threatened in their daily work by the practical managers' resentment about financial inequality, had extracted the most obvious offending characteristic—lack of formal education—and developed a stereotyped reaction to it. They then tried to alleviate their professional insecurity by expressing contempt and distrust for the helpless staff, whom they were free to kick in the managerial hierarchy.

PARALLEL LIVES   In many complex organizations people with different skills and training lead parallel lives. Different groups work side by side without ever meeting. This close but untouching course contributes to fears and resentments. It is as if one group were driving a truck down a freeway at the maximum speed, with another group driving a small sports car alongside at exactly the same speed. After a few miles those in the truck begin to feel threatened by the sports car's proximity; they fear a collision at the slightest curve. The tension builds until those in the truck grow so resentful that they swerve to run the little car out of the way.

Such parallel patterns in organizations breed threats to security and personal dignity. When the majority group is threatened, minority groups are threatened in turn. For example, management can play two competing unions against each other by carefully developed parallel work patterns. Before long the unions forget their common purpose in the suspicion and resentment that grow from working in these alienating circumstances.

Whether you are devising a plan for fomenting dissension or looking for a solution to present disorders, one place to check for prejudice is separation according to educational and financial strata. In the case of the Ph.D.s and the practical managers, one of my recommendations was to integrate the two groups in their daily work, so that their parallel lives intersected. When work patterns offer a variety of opportunities for working together toward common goals, prejudice dies a natural death.

Any attempt at integration must be undertaken with some thought for each group's natural interests. If it is imposed hastily by an outside authority, it can have effects more disastrous than parallel work patterns. If group integration is part of your manipulative plan, you must disguise your real purpose. Act as if you have found a more efficient way of achieving a common goal. If you support the integration with work incentives—pay raises or improved working conditions—the new work force will soon discover that all its members have skills that are essential to high productivity. Before long they will be socializing and drinking together and one manager will say to another in surprise. "Some of my best friends are research people."

THE DIFFERENCE FACTOR   Prejudice arises when a distinguishing characteristic common to a group is isolated and emphasized to the exclusion of all others. People can be conditioned to feel that any characteristic is undesirable. I have seen office forces tear people apart if they deviated from the standard in any way. "She's one of those who wear slacks to work." "He smokes in the men's room." Any innocuous trait may become abhorrent to people who are looking for a helpless dog to kick, an insecurity blanket to fondle.

When you hear people being grouped according to a difference factor, you have a prejudice point to work with. Whether you want to cultivate the difference or alleviate it depends on your manipulative plan. Later in the chapter we will talk about specific kinds of prejudice and ways to control them.

THE MAJORITY URGE   All of us need companionship. We will adjust our behavior drastically to be accepted by people we think are the happiest, strongest, or most successful—whatever quality we hold dear. Majority values, then, become those of people who want to belong. Whether their goal is membership in the country club, voting rights in the union, or a pad in the commune, people sacrifice individual thought for membership privileges.

To protect its position, the majority scorns those who are different. When you spot a difference factor, you should look behind it to see what standards the majority is imposing that makes the difference offensive. In the Ph.D. example, the majority managers began to devise stories about the stupidity of the Ph.D.s. They translated Polish jokes into Ph.D. jokes and told them among themselves. The jokes gave them a sense of security and made them more insensitive to the three Ph.D.s.

Since the department could not have functioned without some highly trained theorists, it was impossible to get rid of the Ph.D.s, but the majority attitude was almost as brutal. "They cause us nothing but trouble. They think they're something special, and all they do is sit around and pretend to think," the managers said to anyone who would listen to their resentment of the Ph.D.s.

When you are seeking a prejudice point, try to uncover the source of majority opinion. Look beneath the ethnic stories, the seething resentment, the contempt, for the real cause of the majority's excuses: "It's better this way. They like staying in their own place. They're not built to do any more than they're doing right now."

The ultimate sign of prejudice, of course, is the "we-they" distinction. Listen to any conversation, with the majority or with the minority, and you will hear the key to prejudice perpetuation. Everyone has accepted the pattern of separation. When you hear the arbitrary division of humanity into two parts, you have heard prejudice at its simplest level.

Playing the Prejudice Field

Prejudice is often disguised as a virtuous action that will enrich life. But as any elementary moralist will tell us, this richness is deceptive, an illusion of self-righteous superiority. True prejudice, in its separating power, is life-limiting. It denies both the recipient and the initiator experiences that would be beneficial.

Deploring prejudice will not make it disappear. Fuzzy-headed social reform will produce only a euphoric sense of self-satisfaction that can be as destructive as prejudice. Remembering the five prejudice points, you can devise manipulative plans for aggravating or taming prejudice. Here are some of the ways to use prejudice to your advantage.

Suppose you are looking for some way of polarizing your department. You happen upon this statistical reality: nine members of the department are under 40 and four are over 40. Since you are under 40, the potential age prejudice works to your advantage. Had you been in the minority, you would have kept quiet and looked for another prejudice point.

You begin by pointing out the "we-they" distinction and work up to more obvious indications of prejudice. In casual conversation you talk about *the others,* the old-timers. You make no derogatory comments at first, but simply point out their separateness. After a few weeks the self-pride on which prejudice is founded begins to surface. You know you are winning when you hear someone say, "Those old-timers think they have the power, but we'll be here long after they're gone."

That attitude is a wonderful one for the majority to cultivate —an attitude of superiority granted by some divine providence working in their favor. From this sense of superiority it is only a short leap to contempt for the disadvantaged minority. If you are in a hurry, you can speed the separation process by selecting some characteristic of older people and mentioning it often. "I'll bet he combs in Grecian Formula every morning," you can say of a man whose hair has remained dark in spite of his age. "They always try to look like us."

Soon gray hair is such an abominable sign of physical inferiority that young people in the office are repelled by it. At that point you add other minority characteristics to your list, playing the difference factor for all it is worth. "I wonder if he has any hair left on his legs. I'll bet they glow in the dark they're so shiny." Hairless legs then become abhorrent too. To these visible signs of weakness you add jokes about prostate trouble, wrinkles, liver spots on the hands, hairs in the ears, and other distinctive minority characteristics.

It won't take much before your ranks begin to swell with pride. Beware at this point. Skillful manipulators are not taken in by their own manipulations. If you actually become prejudiced against gray hair or wrinkles, you lose control of the situation. Many inept manipulators get so caught up in fomenting prejudice that they begin to feel smug and superior. When that weakness strikes, the minority can launch a counterattack so violent that it sweeps the manipulator and friends right down to the unemployment office.

In many organizations people of different ages are physically and professionally separated. Such separation works to the prejudice maker's advantage. If you find someone over 40 working closely and happily alongside a young person, you can easily turn the potentially harmful situation around. You point out that this person is not like other old people. He's almost one of your own kind. Except for such an occasional boundary crosser, you can count on the standard organization process to aid your prejudice manipulation by its parallel-life arrangement.

Once you have exploited the difference factor, the insecurity-blanket and dog-kicking syndromes will automatically come into play. Young people are naturally eager to belong; they are usually paid less than older executives. With these possibilities for insecurity, they will need only an opportunity to kick. Before long the over-40 crowd will have less and less power and your majority group will gain control. When that happens, be careful. Some other shrewd manipulator is probably at work organizing a new minority group that will exclude you from the leadership you've worked so hard to get.

Prejudice: Dealer's Choice

Special kinds of prejudice are the flour out of which the alert manipulator makes dough. Many types of prejudice are present in working situations. Here are a few that you can use to your advantage.

AGE   As we saw in the previous example, young people can manipulate age prejudice to win control. It works equally well in the opposite direction. When the majority is over 40, many kinds of discrimination can be developed against youth. Even in hiring, the young do not have to win out. You can point out their inferiority so clearly that older people are hired to replace the young ones, whose inexperience has made them unsuited for responsible positions in your department.

"Maturity," then, becomes the watchword of your prejudice group. No one would think of replacing a retiree with a young upstart. Experience is what counts. The offensive features for you are the characteristics of the young. Callowness is disgusting. Long hair and bushy mustaches are contemptible. Jeans are irresponsible.

Differences in training too can become prejudice points. Nobody under 40 knows how to spell or how to punctuate a sentence. The young are educated to ask questions instead of give answers. It's almost impossible to talk to them because their vocabulary is so full of slang. Grace and elegance are no longer part of life.

SEX   A particularly active area of prejudice today is sexual difference. Along with age, it is one of the most visible and obvious means of discrimination. Clever manipulators of both sexes are exploiting the occupational unrest now attendant on sexual prejudice.

The bias is not always in favor of the male. In many traditionally female professions where a few men have been hired —library science, elementary-school teaching, and nursing— prejudice against men is widespread. Women, defending their traditional job areas, use stereotyped male characteristics to argue masculine inferiority. Men are gross, rough, incapable of sensitivity, inclined to be impulsive, and brutal in their work.

In male-dominated professions where women are infiltrating in larger numbers—law, medicine, and management—men find numerous discriminatory features to mimic and ridicule. "Let's put full-length mirrors in the corridors so they can see if their slips are showing." "She got fingernail polish all over the computer terminal." "Her hair got caught in the conveyer belt again."

When you plan to manipulate through sexual prejudices, you must be careful that you are not working against a national trend. Now more than ever we are part of a national communications network that works either for us or against us. If you are trying to cultivate an antifeminist attitude in your office and *The New York Times* and *Washington Post* are running articles decrying sexism, you will be fighting a losing battle, or at least a challenging one. It's often wiser to choose a less exploited field where you have more control over the input.

On the other hand, when the media begin an attack, they so frequently go in for overkill that the antifeminist backlash may work in your favor, especially if you are part of a conservative group. It is up to you, the seasoned manipulator, to decide when sexual prejudice suits your particular needs.

CLASS   In some professional situations class differences are the best means of fomenting prejudice. The advantage of class over age and sex is its intangible quality. You can make the "we-they" distinction almost any way you please. All you have to do is to suggest to candidates for majority membership that they belong in your class.

Class prejudice works both ways. People with their roots deep in the soil are just as easily united against the elite as the aristocrats are in their distrust of the masses. You can depend on finding narrow provinciality wherever people come together to work or play.

In America, especially, you can swing either way, since people are sometimes proud of their "background" and sometimes proud of their lack of it. Check out the local situation, extract the appropriate personality trait for the difference factor, and cultivate scorn for the class that is not worthy of inclusion in your snob group.

Indicators of class vary with time and place. In John F. Kennedy's time shirtsleeves were the hallmark of the government elite. In Nixon's time gray flannel was the ruling garb; daring revolutionists may have worn pinstripes, but never shirtsleeves.

Clothes and haircuts are dependable ways of differentiating class, since people are hesitant to change their style. Social habits too are a good way of marking class differences. How does a person act at a dinner party, a cocktail party? Is he easy, cool, flustered, loud? It could be that he is not one of us. Does she play tennis, swim? Maybe she has not had the advantages of a real managerial type. You should also consider mannerisms and language habits. Does someone say "damn" with the right amount of gentility?

Take in those you want and write your own requirements for

membership in your class-conscious group. If you banish someone to minority status, be sure it serves your purpose. Once you have put a minority stamp on people because of class differences, you need never expect to have them working with you again. To be branded déclassé is at least as heinous as to bear the mark of Cain.

EDUCATION   Whatever your educational level, you can use it effectively as a prejudice point. In most organizations the major educational division is between college and noncollege employees. Educational differences, as we have seen, often mean separation in duties, so that people work along parallel lines rather than overlapping. In such a situation, insecurity and dog kicking are likely to work in the prejudice manipulator's favor.

Conversational habits are a good point of difference for manipulating educational prejudices. George was a member of the noncollege majority working as programmers in a large computer center. The managers above him were college-trained, and regarded themselves as superior to those with less education. George noticed right away that their conversation centered around college experiences—fraternities, lectures, beer busts, college football. Their prejudice was all the more exploitable because they were barely conscious of it. Their interests and superiority seemed natural to them.

George prepared an easy prejudice manipulation. He took the conversational differences as his crucial prejudice point and prepared an attack to make the college managers feel inferior, thus suggesting that a reorganization of responsibility ought to be made on the grounds of experience rather than college training. Like all shrewd manipulators, George cast aside his own self-doubts. He asserted his faith in his natural ability, flouting generations of business practice in a field that equated success with educational level.

Seeing the possibility for natural antagonism among his coworkers, George looked around for the right place to begin. He noticed that one manager pulled his ear with his thumb and forefinger when he was thinking hard about a problem. Another had the habit of rubbing his nose with his forefinger before he spoke. George suggested around the office that these were secret greeting signs between old fraternity brothers. It was the sort of thing college boys did all the time. Soon the programmers were pulling their ears and rubbing their noses in ludicrous imitation of the managers.

Having succeeded with ridicule, George began making other unpleasant comparisons. He contrasted college football, which the managers talked about enthusiastically, with high school football, which most of the men in the computer center had played. College ball was professional exploitation; high school ball was for everybody. College ball was training toward a specialized aristocracy of sport; high school ball was democratic and spirit-building.

This kind of contrast, which can be built out of almost any difference in educational experience, made George's fellow programmers feel superior instead of inferior. They began to resent working for a higher-paid minority that was less suited in every way to manage them than one of their own kind. Before long George began to approach the managers directly, speaking to them in "their language." He mentioned his great tenth-grade Shakespeare teacher and talked about *Romeo and Juliet*. The unthinking college types replied with some comment about their college course in Shakespeare. Those listening to the conversation thought they heard a slightly superior tone from the managers.

If the college managers were at all sensitive to human relationships, they were faced with the problem of trying to filter out memories of their college courses and think back to the ones they had had in high school. Whenever the manager attempted this return to earlier memories, a guilty look—a look of sly suppression of facts—came across their faces. The programmers grew more resentful.

The atmosphere in George's office became so pro high

school that even the insensitive managers were making feeble efforts at camaraderie built on shared high school experiences. Again, the managers had to leap over college memories to recall their high school years, thus giving the high-school-educated majority a continuous advantage.

After two years of singlehanded prejudice manipulation, George succeeded. Conditions in the computer center became so belligerently divided between the programmer majority and the management minority that upper management asked for an investigation of conditions. The consultant brought in to study the situation saw that it was too late to smooth over the antagonism. The only solution was widespread firing of experienced workers. Then he had a better thought. Why not take the natural leader and make him section coordinator, a general supervisor over both programmers and managers?

By the time the consultant finished his investigation, he knew that George was the only man for the job. He also knew, but told no one, that George was the instigator of the conflict. The consultant was experienced enough in human relations to know that the person who had initiated the prejudice was the only one with the influence to resolve it satisfactorily.

George got the reward he deserved for having developed the high school–college antagonism: he had to work it out. As the consultant suspected, he was smart enough to bring concord into the area as long as he was being paid more than the college managers to do it.

PROFESSIONAL TRAINING   As we saw in the section on sneer groups, work experience is a rich area for the prejudice maker because professional jealousies abound. In many hospitals the chief of staff has to spend most of his time assuring one surgeon that another is not trying to cut him up, so to speak. Surgeons sneer at anesthesiologists; anesthesiologists sneer back. Everybody sneers at dermatologists, and nurses have their own pecking order.

With this culture medium the prejudice maker can develop a

poisonous virus. In most organizations professional jealousies are undirected. Once you see their potential you can channel them to your advantage, just as George did with his college prejudice.

Don't get your fire so hot, though, that you burn down your organization. When the mix is very rich, with prima-donna personalities and persistent tensions, a touch of prejudice can ignite a blast. Test the atmosphere for gasoline content before striking your match. That rule holds whether you are in a hospital or a petroleum company.

ETHNIC AND REGIONAL DIFFERENCES   Although ethnic prejudices exist in every organization, they are so obvious that only the crassest and most inexperienced manipulator would think of exploiting them. A dentist doesn't use a jackhammer to drill for a cavity; a good manipulator doesn't use ethnic prejudice to manipulate for advancement.

Even here, of course, exceptions arise. Black executives in a white organization cannot ignore the possibility of prejudice toward them. And they naturally want to turn that prejudice to their advantage. At the same time, minority representatives must control their own resentment against whites. Unless they free themselves of hatred, which serves no useful manipulative purpose, they will harm their chances for advancement.

One indication of ethnic prejudice is the imitation of regional accents. It is very easy to ridicule a minority threat by mocking variant pronunciations. Subtle, sophisticated manipulators leave such grossness to less experienced imitators, whose heavy-handed efforts more often gratify their own egos than contribute to responsible manipulation.

To this general prohibited area belong gay jokes, Polish jokes, Jewish jokes, and any other prejudice indicators that exploit ethnic or regional differences. If you are in the habit of participating in ethnic humor in your private life, you should make an effort to exclude it from your professional life. It serves no manipulative purpose and often desensitizes you to the more delicate areas of prejudice manipulation that can be so rewarding.

Prejudice Protection

The single best protection against a prejudice attack is knowledge of prejudice patterns. If you have read this chapter, you should be well armed against such an attack. All that remains is for you to consolidate your knowledge so that you control any attempts at prejudice manipulation. You will want to know the indicators—the symptoms that predict such an attack—and the choice of responses you have to it.

Prejudice attacks are usually conducted against a minority group rather than against a single person. Although you may sometimes be a minority of one, most of the time you will be lumped in with a small group that becomes the object of the attack. You should know, first of all, to what groups you belong in your work situation.

Review the Five-Point Prejudice Guide and find out where you stand. If you are clearly in a minority, determine what degree of friction exists between your group and the majority. Many of the prejudices will be minor, but in times of increased tension they could become full-scale attacks. Be alert to that possibility.

Two subtle indicators of active prejudice are *seemingly* motiveless hatred and *seemingly* irrational responses. Few actions are truly motiveless or irrational. If you shrug your shoulders and say you can't understand, pretty soon you'll be neck-deep in prejudice.

Take motiveless hatred. When one person is brutal to you in a single exchange, it is possible that your attacker had a bad night. When several people, for no apparent reason, seem to despise your actions over a prolonged period, you are looking at hatred generated from prejudice. You had better begin doing some investigating. Find out whether you are the single victim of a scapegoat scheme or whether you belong to a minority group that is going to be offered up for kicking. Most likely, one group, with an active leader, has targeted your group for prejudice.

Most of the time this hatred is undirected—an unconscious response to some situation—and can be remedied with quick action on your part. In more serious situations a manipulator is using you to advance his own purpose. Try to figure out what you are doing that marks you as a member of a minority and elicits irritation from the majority. The irritant could be anything from the way your eyes slant to the way your nose is shaped. Most of the time, at least in business situations, it is something less inevitable than physical features.

Sometimes it is the way you wear your hair or hold a pencil. From time to time I have encountered anti-lefthandedness. When I pick up a pencil to write, an observer feels constrained to comment that lefthanded writing is "abnormal." Nothing is too simple to cause a threat to the smugness of the majority. Insecurity blankets can be woven of almost any material. Knowing when you are a threat is the best protection.

When you have singled out both the obvious and the subtle indicators of prejudice, you are ready to develop your response to it. You have two options: passive acceptance and counterattack. The one you choose depends on the gravity of the situation and your evaluation of its potential harm.

PASSIVE ACCEPTANCE   Passive acceptance is a common response among minority groups. Its weakness is its failure to recognize that prejudice thrives on success. The more you withdraw, the further the majority will push you. Perhaps, when the majority-minority lines have been drawn, you will marshall your forces for counterattack; but the hatred and dog kicking will be so ingrained in members of the insecure majority that they will destroy you before they admit they are wrong.

In spite of the weakness of passive acceptance, certain situations demand it, at least until you have a chance to determine a better way out. While you play the passive role in a minority situation, spend as much time as possible trying to allay the majority fears. Keep your minority characteristics in the closet as much of the time as possible.

Do not spend all your time with the minority at the expense of participating in majority activities. Acquiescence to segregation and parallel living simply intensifies the feeling of difference. Insofar as possible, join the majority. In short, don't wear a pink triangle or a yellow star.

Still, no matter how accepted you feel, don't be deceived. The majority may have suppressed its hatred and dog-kicking instincts; but until the tension-making situation has been eradicated, you are an endangered species. Deceive the majority with your similarities if you can, but never deceive yourself. The irrational rage is still smoldering, and at the first opportunity you will be the victim of a purge.

COUNTERATTACK   Until recently American minorities have accepted their passive, suffering roles. In the last ten or fifteen years the national temper has changed, and minorities have begun launching violent counterattacks. Although this counterattack system may be sanctioned at the national level, it can be destructive in organizations. In your office you don't have federal protection against your inferior status. If you are in a minority you have to assume that you are expendable. When the lines are drawn, you will be the first to go. The best you can count on is a feeling of guilt among members of the majority. The guilt can slow your pursuers while you make uneasy alliances with other minority groups and prepare your defense.

The counterattack can take one of three forms: majority split, majority reversal, or minority dominance. In each case, your purpose is to control the situation in spite of the prejudice against you. If you can stabilize the threat, you will suppress the prejudice for a while. But it could rise again at another tense moment.

In a *majority split* you seek out subversive or minority groups in the seemingly monolithic majority and then set them squabbling among themselves instead of persecuting you. This action is particularly appropriate in a complex organization with numerous competitive or antagonistic units. A quick shield will divert the fire from your minority while you look around for more permanent cover.

Terri, for example, was the only female lawyer in her firm. She was constantly being given tedious work and excluded from the largely masculine conversations at coffee and lunch. With as much wit as malice, she listened to the conversation of this mass majority and gradually perceived a difference of regional accents. By sowing small seeds of regional prejudice in her conversations with her colleagues, she soon created antagonisms that caused several of the lawyers to include her in their new minority which, because of its newness, was a more threatening one than the male-female split.

In a *majority reversal* you take the characteristics that distinguish your minority and glorify them in such a way that the difference factor begins to work in your favor. George's lack of education, which was initially a stigma in his job, ultimately earned him a managerial position over those who had scorned him.

Suppose the majority ridicules your group for its stingy, pennypinching characteristics. In your public statements you make it clear that right now this kind of economy is exactly what the organization is lacking. You proselytize among majority members, preaching yours as the true religion. Pretty soon you have converts to pennypinching. You have made the difference factor a desirable characteristic and made your minority the reforming majority.

When your former enemies are the trembling minority, you view their prodigal, spendthrift nature with superior compassion. Be careful, though, that you do not give them significant jobs in your administration. Some among them still hate you violently and would all but sacrifice their own careers to ruin yours.

Minority dominance is a modification of the majority rever-

sal. Instead of trying to convert others to your side, you strive
to retain your minority status while gaining a power position
over the masses that were trying to persecute you. Again you
work with the characteristics that separate you from the majority, but now you suggest that they are unique to your group
and cannot be developed by others. George suggested that his
distinguishing characteristic was freedom from college-in-
duced smugness. Thus he alone was capable of combining the
compassionate understanding of the programmers with the
managerial wisdom of the college-trained leaders.

Billy Carter is an example of the success of minority dominance. He has exploited the stereotyped characteristics of the
Southern redneck—beer drinking, foul language, and laziness
—so that they now mark him as a special kind of person,
worthy of attention and honor. It is simply a matter of attitude.
Let the majority convince you that you are inferior, and you
will be. Convince them that you are something special, and
their insecurity will make them believe you really are.

By glorifying your minority characteristics, you can achieve
a prejudice reversal; you will make the majority feel inade-
quate, guilty, ashamed, and helpless. It is the sort of aggressive counterattack that will make you a master of manipulation. View it as a challenge.

But remember, when you are in control, you must be so fair
and reasonable in your dealings with minority groups that they
can never turn the tables on you as you have done to them.
The wheel of fortune spins continually, but master manipulators are not playing it. They own it.

Persecution Paula

Paula and I were in high school together. When I went to
college, she took a job in a Washington secretarial pool. She
analyzed her situation wisely and used prejudice to advance
her career. Fifteen years after we went our separate ways, I
talked to her in her carpeted office on the executive floor of a
government administration building. She was assistant to the

director in an agency composed largely of highly trained scientists.

JONES: You certainly have done well, for a high school girl.

PAULA: I've done well partly because I'm just "a high school girl."

JONES: What do you mean? Your limitations have become your assets?

PAULA: I suppose you could say that. While I was working in the secretarial pool, I went from one government agency to another as they needed extra help. I saw men who were so stupid that their secretaries had to tell them when it was time to go to the john. The secretaries were making $5,000 a year, and the executives were making $20,000. The difference? The managers were college-educated men and the secretaries were high-school-trained women.

JONES: You mean you were being discriminated against because of sex and education? Two strikes against you. The whole society approved of that exploitation 15 years ago.

PAULA: The "whole society" never approves of anything. They ignore only what doesn't concern them immediately. I knew I couldn't work with the "whole society," but I could work with my own situation. I wanted to work for a single agency. I had learned all I needed from the pool; it was invaluable experience, because I had seen a general situation of male dominance wherever I went.

I took the job with this agency because, of all those I worked for in the pool, it had the most highly educated managers.

JONES: Wait a minute, Paula. Since you had so little education, why would you choose an agency with the highest educational level among its managers?

PAULA: I had seen that it was easier to make persecution work in your favor if the difference of degree was obvious. If a lot of people in the agency had worked their way up through the ranks, I would have had no sympathy at all. I

didn't want to have to grind my way through the masses to get ahead. I wanted the quickest, most efficient way up.

Anyway, when I got settled here, I began to point out the salary discrepancy between the men and the women. That was long before it was the thing to do nationally. I was ahead of my time there. I wasn't resentful, but persistently and quietly I stirred up trouble among the secretaries and other women who worked here. I even wrote a reasonable article for the agency newsletter pointing out that a great deal of talent was being wasted because of masculine superiority and prejudice against noncollege people. I cited a wage scale that I had taken from a report on my boss's desk. He didn't know it, though. He hadn't had time to look at the figures.

To make a long story short, I continued to exploit the bad working conditions, the refusal of men to sympathize with pregnancies, sick children, and menopause. These female things that had been shameful I used for my glory. My femininity was so embarrassing to them that they sometimes tried to pretend I was a man so they wouldn't have to recognize the differences.

JONES: You sound slightly like a conniving woman, Paula. I don't remember you that way from high school. You were quiet and sweet.

PAULA: Two stereotyped features of women, the persecuted minority. I took those two characteristics—quietness and sweetness—and pointed out that they were essential to the smooth functioning of the organization. By the time I stirred up a whole lot of angry secretaries, the boss asked me if I could develop those characteristics and suppress two other stereotyped ones—bitchiness and whining. My first big job was secretarial reorganization. Several male personnel officers had bitten the dust, primarily because of my howling to the other women about the way men had treated us downtrodden martyrs.

After I got this job, I did a lot for women employees,

but I also made things easier in working relations generally. The director liked my work, mostly the quiet way I ran the place. He said it reminded him of the way his mother had run their home. He had five brothers and sisters, but he always felt safe and secure when his mother was managing things.

JONES: So now you run the agency the way his mother used to run his home—quietly and sweetly.

PAULA: I don't take all the credit, but I must say that it's an improvement over the male brutality that existed before.

JONES: Are you stereotyping men as brutes?

PAULA: Only when it serves my purpose to do so. Usually I try hard to see people as individuals rather than as types. They're easier to manage that way.

JONES: Funny, no one in high school voted you most likely to succeed.

PAULA: Why should they? I was the girl who wasn't planning to go to college. I had no future in those days. I was just quiet and sweet, and I've made the most of the very qualities that made nobody notice me in high school.

JONES: Are you bitter about being an uneducated woman, Paula? Do you find much prejudice around here now?

PAULA: Not much. And when I do, I manage to use it to my own advantage.

JONES: I've rarely known a martyr to wear sainthood so comfortably. Your halo hardly shows at all.

12

TRUTH

Using the Ultimate Ploy

VIEWS of reality are constructed around "the truth." Even cynical people secretly yearn to know what actually *is*. Call it Truth, Reality, or the Answer, some absolute value still informs the thinking of our relativistic age. "You shall know the truth," people say, with no knowledge of the original source of that statement, "and the truth shall make you free."

Most totally disillusioned people cannot be manipulated. They have seen through illusions to realize that action leads to equally meaningless action. Most likely though, they are in a commune or a monastery instead of business, so you won't need to worry about them. The ones who are still trying to get somewhere are the truth seekers. You can use their honest dream of an attainable absolute to shape any illusion you choose.

Skilled manipulators, recognizing that conceptions of the truth vary, never commit themselves to any of them. Their manipulative strength comes from the refusal to see truth as a single glowing touchstone for testing everything and everybody. There are, of course, facts; but even these are perceived differently, according to the preconceptions of the observers. Send five reporters out to cover the same story, and you will end up with five different stories.

As a manipulator, you have to dissociate yourself from the truth seekers. You stand outside the brightly lit center of absolute faith where everything is shadowless brilliance. You have looked at the dark edges of the world where flitting shadows highlight and obscure. That vision is your strength. You can bring selected shadows to the bright center and shade the truth as you choose.

Organizations, though, have no time for such philosophic profundities. Along with each procedures manual comes a tacit assumption of direct access to the absolute truth. As you talk with your associates, find the foundation of their faith and adjust your manipulative techniques accordingly. Politicians and actors are skilled players of the truth game you are now learning. They study their audience to discover what techniques will make their truth shine more convincingly than the dark reality "the truth" obscures.

Longing for truth, people tire quickly in their search and settle for some petty idol of their own, which they then name Truth. On their illusion you construct a superior one, superior because you have chosen it knowing that it is not the ultimate word.

At the center of every truth lies the only validation for it: an individual consciousness. In other words, every truth is created by the individual who perceives it. To manipulate, you have to see the truth the manipulatee sees. Communities, fellowships, and organizations are built by people who believe they share the same concept of the truth. They rarely do, and from the unstated differences among them you develop your manipulative plans.

The Truth-Seeking Examination

You discover the center of people's universe by letting them tell you about their priority system. The things they talk about most frequently are the things they think are important in the world. You gradually learn to develop your individualized manipulation procedure from a person's priority system. There is always the possibility, though, that you may be deceived by layers of deception that your subjects have placed over their central truth. If they have been working very long, they may say what they think you or someone else wants to hear rather than what they actually believe.

To filter quickly through these layers of occupational cloudiness, incorporate my Truth-Seeking Examination into your conversations. I have perfected this technique from over 20 years of interviews with executives. In 90 percent of the cases, the examination findings agreed with the executives' own appraisals of their cosmic centers. Here is how it works.

After several trial runs, you get an accurate reading of your subjects' interests by measuring their "conversational expansion." You ask questions of the same general length and complexity about several broad subjects, ranging from business concerns through current events to private life. After each question you measure the length of the response, either by counting the number of sentences to yourself or by checking the time inconspicuously on your watch. Don't let your face reveal encouragement or discouragement as your subject talks. Listen with the same intensity to the answers to all your questions. When you have sifted out the general areas of interest, devise several more specific questions. Before long, with eight or ten questions, you can pinpoint a subject's concept of what is important in the universe.

Suppose your colleague Harry has shown most interest in home repair. You check to make sure a recent repair problem isn't the reason for his expansiveness. His response tells you that he is far more interested in his home than in his job.

Now you question further. You find that Harry is constantly at work installing cabinets, paneling his basement, or changing an electrical outlet. It becomes obvious that his motivation is not comfort but personal security. He does everything out of a need for self-fulfillment, a drive that he cannot satisfy at work or in personal relationships. When he fits a board exactly into place, he has a gratification he can achieve in no other way.

The test questions can be varied to suit each subject and can be adjusted as you evaluate your findings. If you make the questions part of your normal conversation, you will automatically put your investigation into play and get a sense of each person's truth center after only a few conversations. Here are some truth centers you are likely to find, along with techniques for manipulating them to your advantage.

Economics

The central truth for many people is an economic one. "We have to face the facts of life," they say, meaning "We have to make a living, don't we?" Capitalist or Marxist, they are sure that the central fact of life is financial solvency.

Economic realists are divided into several factions. The largest group sees money simply as purchasing power at the individual level. People in this group are easily manipulated by their basic greed. They have become so convinced of the validity of dollar value that they surrender their time, family, and friends to work overtime so they can buy things they don't need. Their concept of the universe is a self-centered one: everyone is a grabber, just as they are, devoted to grabbing as much out of the general till as possible.

A slightly more sophisticated group sees economic truth in terms of the national economy. These people are more interested in their portfolio than in their salary. They have an eye to the national and international money markets and are more inclined to theory and prophecy than to grabbing. They seek money more for its symbolic value than for its purchasing power. They may even incline toward the miserly, because they'd rather have their money than spend it.

Although these theorists are less obviously greedy than their wage-earning cousins, they are still seeking personal gratification through the manipulation of funds. Both groups respond well to any appeal to selfishness. Fear is a large part of their truth. They have heard what happened to Germany in the 1920s with runaway inflation; the thought of the collapse of the present economic system, the dwindling of social security reserves, and tax reform drives them into instant conformity with your manipulative plans. They will endorse the Alaska Pipeline, the Concorde, or the Army Corps of Engineers if they think that will help keep the economy stable.

A third group of economic truth worshipers sees money not in terms of the security or the products it will buy but in terms of power. They are the ones who know that they are more powerful if they control a $3 million annual budget than if they control a $1 million one.

This understanding of the relationship between money and power, which the first two groups are only vaguely aware of, makes the third group the most difficult to manipulate. They themselves are probably skillful manipulators and are alert to recent refinements in the art of manipulation. Still, they are responsive to cold facts and economic tables. Totally unemotional by temperament, they are pushovers for computer print-outs that show marketing trends. Once they have been convinced of the need for a political intrigue or a monopolistic putsch, they will put their power to work to protect and increase the budgets they already control.

Opposed to these first three groups are the neo-Marxists, who hold the present capitalist system in contempt. They don't reveal themselves immediately because they frequently have not admitted the truth even to themselves. You can spot them, though, by their entrenched disgust with the economic system. They wait expectantly for the collapse of the system and the cleansing revolution that will put them on top for a change.

These people are a strange mixture of utter despair and ridiculous hopefulness. They plod away at their jobs, wishing that their organization would go bankrupt, burn to the ground, or come under investigation by the SEC or the IRS—anything to free them from slavery to an economic system they despise. These people are to economic truth what Satanists are to traditional religion: worshipers of the destructive anti-Christ.

What all four groups have in common is the utter conviction

that the center of the universe is financial. They subordinate their interest in the human and the cultural for the mathematical certainty of a financial system. Although they may occasionally participate in charitable causes or patronize the arts, they still view them as necessary adjuncts to the economic center to which they have committed their trust.

Social Forces

The real truth, say others, is social forces. People cannot do anything about the collapse of family life, drug abuse, overpopulation, poverty. These superhuman forces demand submissive allegiance. Their worshipers give them the same measure of fearful devotion that a devil worshiper displays at the mystery of the Black Mass.

Worshipers of social forces realize that economics is a subordinate order of truth. Social change could wipe out economic truth overnight. Advocates of social forces are fatalistic, more pessimistic than the go-getters who are pushing money. Most of the time they submit weakly. They can be recognized by their dour countenances and their joy at disaster. They are prophets of doom. Whenever a change occurs, they know it is the prelude to disaster.

Threats don't touch these people. They have spent their lives with disaster. The most effective approach with them is a combination of collusive scheming and deception. They know that when the apocalypse arrives, it will not destroy everyone. The ones in the shelters will be saved. The hills will not fall on those with stormcellars. The bomb will spare those who belong to a survival club in the Rockies. Readiness is all.

Underneath their despair lies a sly conviction that they are going to last. They will spend money and effort to separate themselves from the masses, who are doomed to destruction by violent social change. They believe the right school will save their children, the right counselor will save their marriage, the right psychiatrist will save their sanity, and the right church will save their souls.

These people are receptive even to casual slander because they always expect the worst from others. When they hear that someone has contributed to the destructive element, they are glad. They greet malice with open arms because it reinforces their concept of the universe. Social-forces types are a fellowship of the happily damned.

When you spot people who trust social forces, you have to play the prophet. You can talk about economic collapse or the disappearance of energy supply, but remember that down deep they are laughing a bitter laugh. Laugh along. It's the only way. You both know that when the rest of the world is freezing, you and they will have had the foresight to save some coal for personal use.

At any time, these people are ready to play a scheming trick to survive. If social forces are inexorably marshalled against them, they will at least play while the playground lasts. Take them to cabarets and dance on the grave of Western civilization. It can't hurt anything since nobody is personally responsible for its collapse—so say the worshipers of the social forces.

Political Structure

Some people believe that political structure is the central truth. It can control economics, even social forces. They believe that the present structure, or a modification of it, will prevail. They are compromisers. They will deal, switch sides, and bribe in order to keep their ship of state afloat.

They can be recognized by their political involvement, at the national and local levels, and in their business dealings. They might better be called Structuralists, because they believe in the structure they are part of. They campaign wherever they think it will do them the most good, and they are alert to patterns of power in their organization.

Like the highest type of economic truth lovers, these structuralists are unselfishly committed to something beyond themselves. The structure they take for the truth, though, is larger than a financial one. Their sense of history makes them aware of the pain that went into shaping their organization, whether it is a business or a political system. They are the ones who have the slogan "Established in 1928" engraved on their office stationery.

Within the group are reformers and conservatives—those who believe that a few changes will get us to the perfect structure and those who believe that we have just passed the Golden Age and should turn back. These two subgroups are simply different denominations worshiping the same deity: the corporate entity.

Though their own hopes may never be fulfilled, they will compromise and scheme to stay as near the top as possible. One structuralist commented, "If I thought all the time I had spent at political meetings was useless, I'd go out and shoot myself." What he was doing was affirming his faith with the offer of his life. His creed begins "I believe in the Organization Almighty, maker of me and mine." He will spend time, money, and energy on the structure that supports him.

Working for Standard Oil, ITT, IBM, the White House, is a priestly function. The organization takes precedence over other truths because without the organization the resultant chaos would make all truth false. Consequently, almost any action can be justified if it preserves the integrity of the organization. These people give their morality over to the system. Law students and West Point cadets cheat because they want to be part of that structure they revere. Physicians lie for each other in malpractice suits to protect the integrity of their profession. Government officials steal and murder to protect the honor of the state.

Structuralists fight among themselves almost as much as they fight with others. Industry structuralists see the government as antagonistic to their interests because the business structure is often overshadowed by the government structure. Academic structuralists firmly believe that the university should serve as a model for all others: academic expertise will guide business and government in becoming handmaidens to learning, as embodied in the research schemes established by universities.

The church, a benevolent organization, a profession, even a family, can become the dominant structure in a person's life. Once the single structure is elevated to a position of supremacy, the devotee tries to impose its uniqueness on other, less adequate ones. In working with structuralists, you must first find out what their primary structure is. Then develop your manipulative plan by showing that other structures need revising so they conform to this perfect structure. When you find, for example, that a person is a strong believer in family unity, you can make analogies between the company and the family. These analogies can be slanted to indicate that the company needs more parental authority, more differentiation of responsibility, a new allowance system; anything you want to change can be recommended in terms of a comparison with the family.

Structuralists are best controlled through scheming, prediction, and flattery. They must always be watched carefully, because they are usually consummate manipulators themselves. You may find that they are working a double deal that leaves you out of their structure. The manipulator can be manipulated to his own disadvantage by a shrewder, more devoted structuralist.

Duty

Many people still hold to the nineteenth-century conception of duty as truth. These people are sour-faced and constipated; they have a lot of trouble with their digestion. They often clench their fists when they are talking and make self-conscious gestures. They have an evangelical zeal to judge others by their own truth.

Duty worshipers are readily recognized by their fanatical self-righteousness. Knowing what their duty is, they also presume to know what duties should be assigned to the rest of the world. Their conversation consists in large part of judgmental words such as "appalled," "shocked," "aggrieved," and "amused," depending on the gravity of the breach of duty being ferreted out.

They control other people by demanding conformity to the rules, which they know many ways to avoid and bend. They are petty legalists who will get by with anything that is not specifically prohibited. One duty worshiper once said at a staff meeting, "I shall certainly continue to take advantage of this situation as long as there is no specific rule against it." He felt no responsibility for determining whether his behavior was harming his department. He had fulfilled his duty at the moment by being a law-abiding participant in the rape of the department's integrity.

At another time, of course, this same proponent of duty is the reformer who sees it as his duty to speak out against the moral degeneracy around him. His duty varies to suit his personal needs.

Not all duty worshipers are so afflicted with self-interest. Many of them are selfless in their willingness to abide by duty as they see it. Whether they are using duty or bowing down to it, they are certain that the only way to truth is through devotion to some clearly designated responsibility.

These people expect a lot from others. They not only regard their duty and other people's as a serious need; they also ascribe responsibilities to organizations. They may be conservatives who think the organization should make more money for the stockholders or liberals who believe the organization should encourage unionization and minority hiring. Conservative or liberal, these dutiful types are prescriptive in their thinking. They believe government has national and international responsibilities and that salvation comes when these duties are fulfilled.

Underneath this respect for duty lies a deep layer of corporate guilt. They are heirs of the world's failure to worship duty in spirit and in truth. If the White Men had conceived their burden more wisely, we would have eliminated race problems.

If the farmers had not been greedy, there would have been no dust bowl. Wise management of immigration would have saved our cities.

This sense of guilt, combined with their rigid concept of duty, is the starting point for your manipulation. Remind duty worshipers of past failure and they become tractable. Engage their interest and cooperation by suggesting that someone is not accepting personal responsibility. You can lead them around behind you by showing them what they must do in order to fulfill their duty. Once you make them see their responsibility, they are yours.

Fear also is a good way in. Duty worshipers are constantly afraid that they will fall short of their responsibilities. You can predict dire consequences if they don't do something; chances are, they will fall into line. They make wonderfully dependable collectors for the United Fund and office Christmas presents.

Progress

Pure scientists believe in progress as the ultimate truth. They are willing to sacrifice family, job, and life for the advancement of science. But their god is not really science, even though they may say so; it is advancement itself. Science is not a static discipline. It cannot stand still. Progress is what counts, no matter what direction or form it takes.

The idea of getting on has permeated our society. The scientific method is popular because it assumes we are getting better and better, learning more and more. The strength of progress is its close relationship with time: we move forward in time; certainly, then, we also move forward in other ways.

Progressives who work for an organization like to believe that it too is improving as it moves along. They see themselves as part of a great wave of goodness spreading over the world. They know they are better than their fathers because the gross national product is higher than it was a generation ago. They assume that their children will live in a world where expansion continues to dispense its blessings.

Progressives are of a mild and happy disposition. Unlike the constipated advocates of duty, they have no elimination problems. They are optimistic, even in the face of repeated failure. They take the long-range view. A recession strengthens the national will; it is a blessing in disguise. Starvation takes care of overpopulation; India will be better off in the long run.

People of this denomination have to be watched carefully because they are capable of selfless acts. They can be quite quixotic if they believe that what they are doing is for progress. Easily manipulated by arguments for improvement and advancement, they are totally unscrupulous and heartless if they see someone standing in the way of advancement. "Old-fashioned," "outmoded," and "antiquated" are words that turn them into steely-eyed antagonists.

Any technological innovation, no matter how ridiculous, attracts them. A computer or closed-circuit TV thrills them. Suggest sending interoffice memos by satellite, and they will give you seed money to investigate the possibility. Anything will win their approval as long as it involves complex technological change or is classified as experimental.

By collaborating with statisticians and technologists you can demonstrate to them that almost any program is going to contribute to a 17 percent annual increase in something. No progress worshiper ever argues with statistical proof.

Self-Fulfillment

Some people worship at the shrine of self-fulfillment. Unlike the selfless progressives, who truly believe that what is good for the company is good for them, the self-fulfillment types are out for themselves. They are looking for a job where they can feel needed and wanted, a job that will give them personal gratification. They rarely hold positions of importance; but when they do it is usually because they believe organizational advancement is part of personal growth.

These people have no permanent goals. Momentary gratification is all they seek. They will do anything to obtain personal fulfillment. These egoists use themselves as the measure of all things. They can be seen on the handball court or tennis court perfecting their strokes. They are brutal to themselves and others in those areas where they want to improve. They feel perfectly free to change to some new preoccupation without notice. As was said of one of them, "His convictions are sincere but nimble."

Their conversation consists of dialogues about their private lives and public successes. Since they have massive egos that need constant bolstering, they are most easily handled with flattery. They will take large doses of gush. Anything short of continuous praise is antagonistic. Of course, they usually disguise themselves for business purposes, but while they are praising one truth you can see them shifting to another. Their self-deceit is as great as their ego. Their only consistency is their constant focus on themselves.

These people respond easily to suggestions for ways of fulfilling themselves. If you want to get rid of them, just hint several times that they have sold themselves short. Even though they have two Ph.D.s, you can suggest that they are undereducated for people of their intelligence. They will probably run off to school again.

Tad is a typical example of the self-fulfilling type. He began as a scholar who sought truth from the ancients until he finished graduate school. Then he decided that true fulfillment would come through practical application of his academic discipline. He leaped from one minor executive position to another, milking from each the sweetness of budget control and reorganization.

He left each project a shambles that someone else had to come along to clean up; but he was ineffably personable, so jovially convincing that his new interest was *really it* that he continued to hop successfully from spot to spot. He was finally nailed by an administrator who stopped to ask what he had ever accomplished over the past ten years. Tad laughed happily and said that he had enjoyed every minute of his time with the company, but he had a fine opportunity to return to his first love—the classroom. Now he finds fulfillment by telling sophomores how empty and shallow administrative tasks are compared with the joys of teaching.

You will find it difficult to like these people because they like themselves so much. They will come close to antagonizing even the most seasoned manipulator with their rank smugness. Their truth has already freed them from any need for external guidance. They are their own people, they say proudly. Nothing beyond them matters at all. Still, fatuous flattery will get you their attention and support.

Moral Values

Moral values are the highest form of truth for many people. Though moralists have some of the characteristics of duty worshipers, they are narrower. They apply their personal value system to every situation. Like the self-fulfilling types, they bring their private world into the professional one. Their rigidity gives them great assurance. They have no doubts about the right course. Their moral code has an answer for every question. An extremely complex business situation moves them to draw an appropriate thought-stifling cliché from their collection of stale quotations.

Their moral decisions are usually translated from private morality and are ill suited to professional situations. Moralists are constantly seeing similarities between personal relationships and organizational ones. "Atlantic Shipping is our great friend," "Transcon can't be trusted," "We owe U-Travel a debt of gratitude." They run their professional life as if it were a personal matter.

The only place to meet moralists is on their own ground. If they argue morality and you oppose them, you are the immoralist. It is easier to trade moral dictums with them. If they say we owe U-Travel a debt of gratitude, you say the debt has long been paid. If they say Transcon can't be trusted, you point out that morality requires us to give new management another chance. As for Atlantic Shipping—friendship has its responsibilities too.

Moralists are a popular type in administrative circles. The simplicity of their thinking makes it easy for them to get ahead. They are never trapped by moral dilemmas or slowed by intricate logic. A superficial truism will see them through. They speak with great conviction and seldom have to reverse themselves, since their opinions are stated in such general terms that they are almost always applicable.

They have no trouble managing large hoards of people because they firmly believe in the gospel of love. They make high-toned speeches to their staff, outlining their plans in catchphrases that spell kitschy words. CAN is a lecture on checking all negotiations. BEST is a four-point program for improvement: beautify, estimate, stabilize, and transport.

Moralists are cruel and heartless. They can afford to be because of their righteousness. If you violate their code, you have no rights because you have rejected your humanity. Like the Spanish Inquisitors, moralists turn heretics over to the secular arm to be burned. Manipulating them is a dangerous game. They will slash and malign. And their vengeance is permanent. A moralist never forgets.

Religion

Many business executives have an active religious life and believe that religion is the center of existence. Some of these people have difficulty translating biblical truths into professional situations. They protest that Christian love is the basis of their lives, but their total lack of forgiveness and their vicious inability to see other points of view does not give them a Christlike image. One executive who told people that Jesus was his model for life saw no contradiction in then saying that he hated nearly everybody in his department.

The few people who actually pursue biblical truth cannot be manipulated. True followers of Christ's teaching will, like their master, see the purpose under the surface. But most of those who protest their religion loudly are using it for selfish advancement or because it is a socially acceptable pattern of behavior.

For the ones whose religious truth is superficial rather than actual, an ability to quote biblical verses and sermons will help you advance your purpose. Since our culture is traditionally Christian, the nominal Christians have a small storehouse of phrases to live by. Learn the Ten Commandments, the Golden Rule, and the story of the Good Samaritan and you know as much as they do.

With this information, plus a few Old Testament stories, you can argue as well as they can. Usually, after some superficial sermonizing about the importance of love, these people will reveal another, deeper truth. Then you can go to work on them by manipulating that underlying belief.

Truly Trudie

Trudie has worked for 25 years as secretary to the president of a large industry. She is always pleasant, always firm about appointments, and never loses her temper. No one can ever remember seeing her with a hair out of place or hearing a tremor in her calm, sure voice. I talked to her one afternoon between her incoming phone calls.

JONES: You must have to deal with a lot of different types of people in your job.

TRUDIE: They're different on the surface, but down deep they're all the same.

JONES: What do you mean?

TRUDIE: They all want something. Some of them get it, and some of them don't.

JONES: Could you make any guesses about which ones get what they want?

TRUDIE: Sure. I can tell the winners from the losers by the time they tell me who they are. On the phone or through that door, it's the same thing. The winners have an energy that the losers don't.

JONES: How do you see the energy? Do the winners come in waving their arms and laughing a lot?

TRUDIE: I don't mean that kind of energy. I mean a concentrated awareness of what's going on, combined with a way of listening and looking that suggests they see you as a person.

JONES: The winners look and act alike, then?

TRUDIE: No. Some are loud, some quiet, some happy, some sad. What they have in common is a confidence that they're going to make it. They're interesting. I guess that's it.

JONES: Interesting to you?

TRUDIE: Yes, because they're interested in things around them. They're putting things together all the time. You can see the wheels turning while they're talking to you.

JONES: What do you think makes them interested—and interesting?

TRUDIE: I guess they're honest. I don't mean that they tell the truth all the time. They're realistic about themselves and the world around them. They don't try to fool themselves or other people. They may have to deceive occasionally and manipulate, but they don't ever lose sight of the really energetic truth pulsing under all the fakery.

JONES: So you think truth makes the difference?

TRUDIE: I'm sure of it.

13

STYLE

Applying the Final Polish

ONE SPRING I was in Washington when the azaleas and rhododendrons were in bloom. The old houses along Massachusetts Avenue were banked with pinks and reds, blooming against the melting patches of late snow. I came home to the Midwest and spent my consulting fee on azalea and rhododendron plants. After two years of struggling with pH adjustments and special fertilizers, I got one bloom out of a rhododendron. The azaleas were not so successful. A friendly botanist said to me, trying to keep the pitying laughter out of his voice, "Jones, you should learn to work with nature, not against it. Grow peonies."

I have taken only half of his advice. I don't grow peonies, but I have learned the importance of working with nature, not against it. As a matter of fact, that piece of botanical wisdom is the secret to applying the final polish to the manipulative process.

You have now learned the rudiments of manipulation control. It remains for you to shape these generalizations to your own style of manipulation. You have a unique personality, formed by your background and special blend of experiences. Out of this uniqueness grows the style you need to manipulate successfully. Use somebody else's style, and you'll be lucky to get one bloom in two years. Let your own find its natural expression, and you'll be growing azaleas in Siberia.

Style is evident in every manipulation you undertake. Either you bungle through it awkwardly, or you do it with such elegance that even your manipulatees give you a grudging compliment: "You certainly pulled that one off with style!" After your first fumbling efforts, you discover that some kinds of manipulation are more comfortable for you than others. Like positions for intercourse, you don't know which ones are most rewarding until you've tried them all.

Manipulative skill is not something that just comes naturally. No one brings a scheme off with great sang-froid or éclat without practicing a long time to achieve the illusion of effortlessness.

Manipulation, like piano playing or close-order drill, requires consistent, guided practice. True style in any art comes when you have mastered the individual skills so that you are able to act automatically, almost intuitively. But hard work always comes first. Once you master the basic exercises, you are on your way to the ultimate goal: a self-assured style that is classic in its cool elegance.

This book has provided you with a comprehensive guide to basic exercises. This chapter assumes that you have begun to understand the individual techniques that comprise the manipulative art. You have come to realize that manipulation is not an occasional tool, like a hoe, to be taken off its hook only at planting time. It is a way of life that demands total commitment. Although you may be engaged in active manipulation only a small part of the time, you are always a manipulator—collecting data, seeing patterns, listening to people's conversations.

As your style develops, your sensitivity becomes as keen as that of the lyric poets. And your product can be as beautiful an expression of life as theirs. You are the poet of the marketplace, the bard of corporate life. Like all great creative artists, you stand aloof from society, appraising its possibilities and their consequences. With such a dispassionate attitude and such conscious training, you will acquire the style that puts the finishing touches on your manipulative skill.

Artistic Intention

Style cannot be achieved without constant awareness of purpose and method. At the same time, it cannot be self-conscious. Dancers need to know at every moment where their feet are in relation to their partners'. Otherwise, they will stumble. Yet good dancers never look at their feet. They have to *seem* unaware of them as far as observers are concerned. And they must work so hard at their art that they achieve an illusion of freedom.

Awareness of detail without debilitating self-consciousness is the aim of every stylist. Artistic manipulators practice so diligently that their actions have the inevitability of all great art. No one who watches their performance should ever say, "Wouldn't it be better to do it this way?" The knowledge that they have perfected their skills frees sophisticated manipulators from insecurity and fear, so that they can move with confident steps along the path to fulfilling their goals.

One of Shakespeare's most famous courtiers, Polonius, said, "By indirections we find directions out." That might be the motto for the manipulative stylist of any age, because it so clearly indicates the right approach to manipulative situations. Here is what Polonius meant.

Suppose you are lost in the Colorado mountains and it is growing dark and cold. You set out with frightened haste in a direct route toward the place where you think your campsite is. When you have walked 20 minutes, you turn and walk in another direction, more frightened and determined than ever that you are going to find the camp. You might stumble on it in a few days, or you might end up in Canada or Mexico, or frozen on the peak.

Experienced mountain climbers never take a direct course anywhere. Instead of descending in a straight line, they move fearlessly downhill in massive, controlled curves until they find a stream bed. Then they follow it down to shelter. After a good night's sleep in some rancher's bunkhouse, they let the friendly cowboy drive them back to camp in a jeep.

Like experienced mountain climbers, good manipulators do not achieve their intention by bull-headed driving in one direction through briar and thicket. They feel out their environment and follow the natural markings to the goal they are sure they will find. Hesitation, insecurity, self-doubt set fainthearted manipulators off in a frantic dash in any direction. Manipulators who have studied the basic techniques move in stylish curves across the rough terrain until their purposeful indirections find directions out.

Intentions, to be useful, have to be in the realm of reality, not of dreams. Knowing your strengths and weaknesses, you select carefully those devices most appropriate for your manipulative plans. Dreaming can occasionally be a stimulus to action, but it is no substitute for honest appraisal of your situation and your manipulative skill. When you learn what is appropriate to both, you will manipulate others with success—and style.

Appropriateness

Unless we are totally insular and insensitive, we are conditioned by our human contacts. Past experiences shape our desires and how we go about fulfilling them. The people around us show us what we want. We then develop a style to conform to what the people in our immediate manipulative environment have come to regard as stylish.

Style does not exist in a vacuum; it is determined by our taste and the taste of those people we wish to influence. We don't speak to the minister the same way we speak to our children or our friends. If we work with a group of low-key bankers, we do not achieve our artistic intention by shouting. In the holy sanctuary where money is always present, hushed tones are appropriate for manipulation. Selling beer at a ball game would require a different voice.

Suiting your manipulative pressure to the occasion is a crucial area of style. What you have already learned about different kinds of manipulatees will help you when you consider appropriateness. Many inexperienced manipulators do not consider appropriate style as seriously as they should. As a result, they select insulting techniques that infuriate their manipulatees with their obviousness.

Tom is a notable example of an unstylish bore. When he was in high school, he talked one of his old-maid English teachers out of flunking him by stopping by to "visit with her" once or twice a week after school. The woman was so flattered to have a charming young man paying attention to her that she agreed to give him a passing grade.

When he got a job selling real estate, he worked directly under an extremely efficient, self-confident businesswoman who expected her agents to bring in a sale at least once a week. The first two times that Tom failed to make a sale, he hung around after work to charm his new lady grader. She was patient and understanding with him but anxious to get back to work.

The third time Tom leaned over her desk and leered at her with the vestige of his high-school-hero smile, she was blunt. "Why don't you go out and try some of that grease on the customers?" she said. "It doesn't go with me."

Tom decided she was trying to hide her true emotions and made a quick pass at her. She fired him. His error? He had assumed that the manipulative technique that was right once was always right. His arrogant insensitivity let him generalize from one success: because charm had worked on one woman it was the manipulative approach for all women. More sensitive stylists would have traveled by indirection toward their objective until they understood it thoroughly.

Confidence such as Tom's can be easily misplaced. The degree of confidence that manipulators demonstrate and the way they demonstrate it are crucial to smooth manipulation. Just as hushed tones are right for one occasion and loud pushing for another, so every aspect of style is determined largely by circumstance. Until you understand the people you want to manipulate, you cannot know with any degree of accuracy how much confidence to display. Here are some examples to show you how to succeed with any style, from high-pitched to low-key.

BRASH AND ARROGANT   Certain manipulative situations require a style that can best be described as brash and arrogant. With some audiences anything short of brutal bluster is taken for weakness. The forcefulness of your subjects will let you know when you have to project brassy loudness.

If your subjects are loud and crass, you have to respond in kind. You tell filthy stories, recall recent graffiti; you adjust your humor to match that of the standup comic you once saw on TV and quickly switched off.

You have no choice but to respond to loud people with a style matching their own arrogance. Almost any other approach is an insult to their crudity. Once in a while you can attempt a contrast and be calmly arrogant, with steel-blue coolness instead of white-hot loudness; but you need superskill to switch moods with brash and arrogant people, because they usually have a single-value orientation. Unless the rest of the world conforms to their pattern, it is a threat or an insult. Either reaction can upset a manipulator unless it is carefully controlled.

PATRONIZING   Closely related to brash arrogance is the patronizing tone people take with inferiors. It is a style that can easily backfire and should not be used unless you are sure that it will be effective. It consists of rather obvious flattery and works best with the lonely and downtrodden.

This is the tone Tom used to talk his high school teacher out of flunking him. His youth and masculinity gave him a sense of superiority that he used to charm the old woman. And it worked.

Tom was only lucky, though, not skillful. For patronizing to work, the recipient must really accept the manipulator's higher position and not resent it. Use it with equals or superiors, and you will be upset by violent rebellion, as Tom was when he tried his masculine strength on the real estate saleswoman.

SELF-ASSURED   For most manipulative situations it is best to adopt a calm, confident manner and to choose your words carefully. Some managers find this approach too subtle; but it is the one that sophisticated manipulators favor, since it has the lowest risk and the highest return. Most people in managerial positions know that has-beens talk about what they did in the Indiana plant ten years ago and fakers talk about the Great Project they have under consideration by a major funding agency.

Self-assured manipulators—the ones with competence and promise—say little. When they do speak, it is to the immediate situation. They are confident they can handle any problem that arises, but they are not certain how long it will take until they examine the situation more thoroughly. Their positive approach to life is expressed in a reasonable optimism that enables them to relax at interviews, even when the tension rises.

Arrogant and patronizing manipulators use conversation as a vehicle to convey their accomplishments to others. Self-assured manipulators talk about the situation rather than about themselves. They take their basic worth for granted.

I do not mean to glorify the self-assured approach over the others. In some situations arrogance is the preferred manipulative style. One man I know tells everyone what a great administrator he is, how he has turned a declining earnings picture around in a matter of months with his shrewd handling. Although most people laugh at him and his foolish posturing, this pompous ass has gained more support from his superiors than all the self-assured realists who preceded him. In this case, arrogance works where quiet assurance has failed repeatedly. The pompous ass does not care who laughs as long as he is presenting the right stance to the people whose support he needs.

There is no general rule about when a stance is appropriate. Self-assurance is simply the best neutral position to assume until you discover what your manipulatees regard as the visible signs of confidence and power. When you know that, you can shift to the stance they expect from a winner.

HUMBLE   Some people still believe the old saw that the best administrators don't want the job. In dealing with such people —the ones who protest loudly that they don't have real power, they just work for the organization—you should blend self-assurance with occasional fits of humility. Even though self-effacement is not a winning approach in the long run, it can be extremely effective when placed momentarily against brash arrogance.

Humble manipulators are not silent. They belittle their own ability, protesting that they are well meaning but are not as valuable as other people in their department. The best time to use the humble approach is when an arrogant opponent is making a play for a position you don't want. The power play will take so much time and thought that your opponent will be put into dry dock for the next ten years while you work out into the main channel and steam ahead.

Each of these manipulative styles is appropriate for some situations and inappropriate for others. Manipulators cultivate versatility by shifting from one style to another without appearing insincere or inconsistent. Like great singers who move from one register to another with no break, skilled manipulators move effortlessly from level to level of self-confidence as the shifting tides of manipulation swirl around them.

Remember, your goal in manipulation is not to project your own mood; it is to create the mood that is appropriate for the occasion and expected by your manipulatees. Disappoint your audience, and you lose your manipulative power. Versatility, flexibility, and sensitivity to your audience's taste will assure you of a winning style.

The Culture-Hero Taste Test

As a manipulator, you have two audiences. The first is the manipulatee, for whom you act as director, coaching the subject in a role that suits your purpose. Then you lead the manipulatee through that role for the second audience, those who are observing the performance. Sometimes the response of the manipulatee is all you have to be concerned with. More often though, your success depends on the reaction of the second audience.

Frequently these two audiences—manipulatee and observers—have different tastes. Consequently, they respond differently to a particular manipulative style. Before you begin your manipulation, you can subject both manipulatee and observers to a taste test to determine what style is appropriate for each stage of your complex production.

The style your subjects respond to best depends on their culture heroes. These heroes, selected from the masses of people they meet and read about, take a special place in their personal mythology. They ascribe acts of superhuman achievement to them; their best efforts are only a pitiful shadow of their legendary heroes' deeds.

Until you know whether a subject admires Thomas Jefferson, Mick Jagger, or Jane Fonda, you can't know what style to present in your negotiations. The culture hero is the physical embodiment of the manipulatee's ideals. The Culture-Hero Taste Test will give you the information you need to develop an approach compatible with your subject's sense of style.

To prepare for the test, arrange a graph with "goof-off" at the bottom, "oafish" directly above it, "practical" somewhere near the center, and "suave" at the top. In between these qualities fill in others that shade into each other. Spend some time talking with or observing your subject. Then put in points on your graph, depending on the answers to these five questions:

1. What people does your subject talk most about, other than his family and himself?

2. When he discusses television and the movies, what kind of personalities does he admire most?
3. As he thumbs through newspapers and magazines, where does his glance linger longest?
4. When you are talking together in a public place, what kind of person does he glance at longest?
5. From his own appearance, how would you rank him on the taste scale?

When you see where your points cluster, select a mythic hero who resembles that style and pattern your style after it. Suppose you find that your subject's hero taste is somewhere between "oafish" and "goof-off." You would select Meathead of "All in the Family" or some other TV oaf. Or you could take Tom Sawyer or Huck Finn, some character that is easy to imitate.

Next, select a *characteristic gesture* and incorporate it subtly into your personality when you deal with your manipulatee. The gesture will help you simulate a style that makes your subject feel at ease. Think of Tom Sawyer sitting in the shade while others do his work, or Huck Finn dangling his feet in the river off the edge of his raft. The mental image of that pose will translate into your demeanor, and your style will ring true.

For other hero tastes, study other models. Watch the way sophisticated people sip a martini or light a cigarette and then meditate on that gesture as you move into your suave style. Actors are excellent subjects for study: they have already extracted from human experience the gestures of the characters they are playing and have enlarged them for their audience's benefit. All you have to do is lift them from the actor's collection and put them into your own.

Of course you do not want to be a ham. Culture-hero reproduction tends to become, in inept hands, parody or ridicule. With a careful choice of model and a good deal of self-restraint, you will play directly into your manipulatee's high esteem if you use the style of his culture hero.

Audience Response

With knowledge of your audience's taste, you will be able to impose a *dominant mood* on your manipulative productions. This mood makes manipulation easier and helps you control audience response.

The dominant mood is composed of tone and atmosphere. *Tone* is the force level at which you implement your manipulative system. Thinking of it in terms of sound, you decide to have a shrill, insistent tone or a low, bass throb. It is controlled by the speed and density of manipulative techniques directed at your subject. The more intensity you put into your manipulation, the shriller the tone becomes.

Atmosphere is the medium through which your audience views the manipulative process. It can range from stormy to calm, foggy to bright, light to dark. You create the dominant mood by changing the tone and the atmosphere.

T.C. knew how to manipulate with style. He came to the department for an interview four months before he was to begin work. He wrote the names and descriptions of the seven people in the department in a black notebook and went away.

During those four months he corresponded with each member of the department. The letters were masterpieces of style. T.C. suggested in each letter that his correspondent was the only one in the department he could communicate with. He hoped that when he arrived they would be able to reshape the department to their own managerial concept.

When T.C. got to the department, he shifted to the oral manipulative style that we have been studying. For each of his seven colleagues he created a special tone and atmosphere, so that each was bottled up inside his own container with his own individual buzzing going on inside his head.

The sounds and the sights of each dominant mood filtered out other sights and sounds so that T.C., by gentle manipulation of the tone and the atmosphere in each of the bottles, could maintain a mood of his own choosing. Sometimes he shook one of the bottles and sent a flurry of blinding sleet through the atmosphere, whipping up a wind that howled around the poor subject's head. The manipulatee shivered and cringed. All the while another manipulatee in an adjoining bottle was basking in warm, windless sunlight. Together the seven bottles played a variety of tunes that shifted from a major chord to a minor one at a gesture from T.C.

Observers from other departments and upper management saw immediately that T.C. was a born leader. "He's got the know-how to make that department work," they said. Soon T.C. had everything running the way he wanted it. The department became a physical manifestation of his own style of management through dominant mood.

Language Styles

Language and audience response are crucial to style. Since we manipulate largely through the spoken word, we must gain control over that medium before we can be at ease with manipulative techniques. Sensitivity to language comes with practice; experienced manipulators are alert to the emotional effects of their words and adjust their tone accordingly.

Suppose you are talking to a manipulatee and happen to say, "What a strange adumbration to this event!" From the momentarily startled look in his eyes, you know that your subject doesn't know what "adumbration" means. You make a note of his particular vocabulary level and use big words with him only when you want to overwhelm him in committee. Remembering his momentary confusion, you lay on the big words at meetings until his confusion confounds him.

Language style is developed by conscious selection of certain types of words in sizable proportions. You can make the most trivial and insignificant subject sound profound by adding the right kind of verbal dressing. In the same way, as long as you know what you are talking about, you can translate a relatively complex matter into simple language for a particular audience.

Sometimes you want to communicate through language; at other times you want to obscure. You need to know what your purpose is in each situation and how to suit your language to the task.

LEARNED WORDS   A learned word is one that is learned after a first word has taken its place in the general vocabulary. The choice of a word like "fortnight" for a two-week period or "inundation" for a flood is a choice of learned over common. These words tend to have ordinary equivalents in general conversation. Learned words are available to anyone who has a desk dictionary, but they are usually employed by a relatively small, educated minority.

Using learned words does not automatically gain you points. In some groups learned words will mark you as gifted and intelligent. In other groups these words are taken for granted, and you are not accepted unless you use high-level, abstract terms. In still other groups the same words mark you as pompous or snobbish.

Special pronunciations can also brand you quickly as either an arrogant snob or a hopeless illiterate, depending on the people you are talking to. The way you say "advertisement," "aunt," "tomato," and "either" can make listeners feel intimidated or superior.

Until you know your audience's tastes, the common words near the center of the vocabulary are the safest. Don't use complex words when simple ones will do. If you have to make a presentation outside your usual group, make a special effort to reshape your material to suit the tastes of the new audience.

The middle-of-the-road style is the best medium for both oral and written communication. When you swerve toward the learned word or the odd pronunciation, you should have a special purpose for doing so: either to impress or to irritate. Otherwise, stay with ordinary usage and make your point without stirring up emotional undercurrents.

TECHNICAL VOCABULARIES   Within every group certain commonly used words develop specialized meanings. "Closing," for example, means something quite different to a real estate woman and to a speech maker. When the politician talks about "intercourse" between nations, the prostitute gets an amusing picture of England and America in action. Humorists trade on the misunderstandings brought about by transferring technical jargon from one profession to another.

Technical words, like learned words, have emotional power. Nothing is more irritating than having to figure out the meaning of an unfamiliar word that a speaker glides over casually with no explanation. "Irrotational flow" may be fine in civil engineering circles, but it needs a footnote anywhere else.

Unless you are intentionally trying to make your subjects feel like outsiders or are trying to intimidate them with your specialized knowledge—two possibilities in manipulation, of course—you should avoid technical terms. They exclude and pollute simple communication with their muddiness.

TRITENESS   Many people hear clever expressions that seem to summarize some common problem and then add the phrases to their own vocabulary. If they are not careful, they will overuse these handy expressions until they begin to sound secondhand and trite. They will even discourage communication rather than encourage it.

When someone says to you, "I'm wearing two hats," he is hiding behind a cliché. What he really means is "I'm so important that I am doing two jobs." These thought stoppers are irritating to thinking people. If you use them, you should have a reason; most of the time such words will mark you as a speaker of nonthink.

Words and phrases rise and fall in popularity. "The thrust of my argument" was extremely clever when NASA rocketry was in vogue. Now the phrase is as moth-eaten as a Salvation Army overcoat. "Simplistic" has been so overused that it has little meaning left.

People who talk a lot without saying anything fill in the blanks in their thinking with clichés; their mouths continue running while their minds idle. Here is a standard triteness expert at work: "I'd like to visit with you for a while to get down to the nitty-gritty and finalize a game plan at this point in time before we open another whole can of worms when the ball is in your court." Translated into ordinary language, this sentence means "Hello."

When you hear others using trite phrases, you're safe in assuming that they have little feeling for words and will be overwhelmed by any serious verbal effort on your part. Treat such people gently. They are linguistically handicapped.

PROFANITY AND SLANG   Profanity and slang are special breeds of triteness, but they are more useful than most trite expressions. Like all specialized word forms, they should be suited to the audience. Learn your subject's profanity pattern and then adjust your style to it.

Is your manipulatee a simple "helluva" type or one of the more colorful "sonuva" breed? Both types are largely unaware of their profanity and rarely differentiate it from the rest of their language. They use these expressions because they once thought of them as daring and dramatic, sort of verbal underlinings. But since they underline nearly everything they say, nobody notices the lines any longer.

These types respond happily to variations on their dull and boring originals. To put style into your profanity, take a poetic approach. Give your listeners new mixtures and compound expressions—a "helluva sonuva" pattern. Or try some variation on the old formula. Depending on your subject's background, you can go for "sonuva Texas rattlesnake," "sonuva Missouri mule," or "sonuva Houston whore." The list is endless once you have broken the pattern of nonthink and made profanity part of your personal style.

You can inject your slang with the same new life. Slang serves no purpose unless you are using it consciously to enrich your style. Learn the standard magic words that your manipulatees use to indicate their membership in a "with it" club that knows "where it's at." Then move on from there.

Profanity and slang are easily imitated, since they are usually simple-minded reflexes that protect people from coping with the complexities of reality. Come in with the usual-plus-one and you have a winning style. Just be sure you do not develop the habit. If slang and profanity become a reflexive part of your thinking, you will be susceptible to manipulation by those around you. And that is the road to destruction.

ABBREVIATIONS AND ACRONYMS   In some circles it is considered stylish to use abbreviated forms of words and acronyms —abbreviations pronounced as words rather than as separate letters. As with other specialized word forms, knowing the meaning of the abbreviation makes people feel like insiders, members of a special club.

You should not disturb this placid sense of belonging without some conscious manipulative intention. When you want to throw your manipulatee off guard, you can invent a new or unexpected abbreviation and throw it into the conversation. By creating a breath stopper, you can cause your victim's eyes to glaze over at the possibility of an unexplored abbreviation.

"She's not OCD," you say and continue your analysis of someone who is not "our class, dear." Or "he's so OTM," you say of a one-track-minded colleague. When such personalized abbreviations are dropped among NASA, NIH, HEW, and CIA personnel, they alleviate boredom and put you one up on stylish abbreviators.

The Language Painter's Color Chart

Manipulators with style practice word games because words are the vehicle for manipulation. Through language they create the dominant moods that suit their purpose. These moods are best considered in terms of colors, from lightest to darkest, depending on the amount of clarity or obscurity they provide the stylist.

Sky-blue is a style made up largely of words drawn from the center of the vocabulary, put together in short, direct sentences, and clearly organized paragraphs. When you choose sky-blue language, you are not trying to confuse but to enlighten. Your language is free of slang and abbreviations and tends toward concrete words rather than high-flown abstractions such as "virtue" and "integrity."

Sunshine-yellow is somewhat brighter and more flashy than sky-blue. It sparkles with occasional flourishes of obscenity or profanity and is ornamented with an appropriately relevant cliché. It creates a sense of familiar reassurance in the listener. Nothing about it is foreign or frightening. Sunshine-yellow sentences are short, strung together with dashes, and occasionally followed by exclamation points. Rhetorical questions raise exciting thoughts and leave them dangling for future consideration.

This style sparkles like summer light on a wind-ruffled lake. It is almost too bright for continuous observation. It is particularly appropriate for flimflam artists.

Papal-purple is richer and darker than sunshine-yellow. It screens out much of the light through stained glass and lets it fall on black velvet rather than white polyester. To achieve this stylish effect, you must think big and abstract: "humankind" rather than "men, women, and children"; "budgetary considerations" rather than "money, sales, and services." You never use a clear, direct word when a fuzzy one will do. The tone achieved is one of sanctimoniousness. It is appropriate for ritualistic occasions such as board meetings where you want to be brilliant but subdued.

Charcoal-gray is an extension of papal-purple. Here all the light has been removed; the stained glass has been replaced by heavy shutters. Your sentences drag on into eternity, qualified by numerous exceptions, limitations, and alternative considerations. Your listeners have to feel their way through your sentences with hands in front of them so they don't bump into some heavy object. You can use learned words, slang expressions. Any mixture of word types is all right with charcoal-gray because your purpose is to complicate and obscure.

These are only a few of the many colors you can choose when you get ready to paint your manipulative mood. Select a color to go with your particular purpose and mix your language to match. Thinking of moods as colors will help you suit your style to your subject matter—and end up with a whitewash for yourself whenever necessary.

Stylish Laughter

Laughter helps you decide whether your style is holding with your manipulatee. You rarely laugh yourself, but you listen for appropriate laughter from your subject. It can be the just reward for manipulation skillfully administered. Laughter, like language style, has countless varieties. Here are a few common laughter responses to look for as you practice your manipulative techniques.

TRUSTING LAUGHTER   The happiest sound in the world for a manipulator is the spontaneous, carefree glee of a victim. It comes whenever your subjects are so thoroughly under your control that they have no fears or worries. You elicit trustful laughter by putting their fears to rest, then driving them easily along a road that takes them where you want them to go.

ONE-UP LAUGHTER   Like trusting laughter, laughter that results from ridicule is an indication of companionship, but it results from a different kind of shared experience. Here you and your manipulatee are sharing a laugh at someone else's expense. When you are working toward alienating people or separating your subjects from their friends, you should definitely work toward this kind of laughter.

You hold up some goal or person as totally worthless. Little by little you point out the ludicrous aspects of the object of ridicule. With parody, satire, and invective you demean it until the only possible response is a superior laugh from those who know the stupidity of the rest of the world and share your contempt for it.

CYNICAL LAUGHTER   When you push ridicule to the extreme, you get a bitter, disillusioned guffaw. Often mixed with tears of disappointment, it is the anguished cry of a spirit that has given up hope of finding meaning in life. You have to listen carefully for it because, like the song of the swan, it is never repeated. When you hear cynical laughter you know that you have triumphed and can continue your manipulation with one more wounded player out of the game. Your victim is convinced that further effort is useless in this dog-eat-dog world.

WINNING LAUGHTER   The toughest kind of laughter to listen to is that of a winner. When you win, you don't laugh; you are too busy planning the next step. When your opponents win, they may give vent to that most hideous of sounds, a winning laugh. If you are an experienced manipulator, you are accustomed to the sound and accept it as part of the game. Your style never shows to better advantage than in the moment of defeat. Lose a battle gracefully and you turn out to be a champion manipulator in the long run.

Seeing It Whole

High style depends, finally, on the ability to anticipate every possible response from your subject. A good way to do this is to rehearse the manipulation in your head beforehand. With the help of the first chapters of this book, you learn how to anticipate possible responses from your manipulatee so that you can incorporate them into your next move. As you grow in manipulative skill and develop your intuitive powers, you will be able to hold the entire manipulative process in your head while you move through it, shaping it to any new response from your subject.

Style comes with this free-flowing movement of a controlled vision. Once you grasp the total manipulative process intuitively, you bridge the alien space between you and the rest of the world with such elegant grace that even your manipulatees admire your style.

One final word. Never put away this guidebook to manipulation. Seasoned professionals keep the rules beside them as they manipulate or watch other skilled manipulators at work. Even now someone may be reading over a chapter that contained a sentence you have overlooked. So from time to time go back again and work out a practice scheme that will help you keep the polish on your manipulative skill.

Straight Sam

Sam had never thought about manipulation as such. The idea offended him, especially when it was connected with a discussion of professional style. I talked with this experienced executive for about three hours one night. Here is the conclusion of our conversation.

SAM: I'll grant you that most people think they're something special. Occasionally I've tried to adopt an opponent's style so that I could argue better, but I'd hate to call that manipulation.

JONES: I notice you're differentiating "arguing" from "manipulating." Isn't it finally the same thing? Techniques for turning an opponent into a supporter?

SAM: I don't feel easy with that term "manipulation." I think you've been misusing it. I debate with people, tell them what they're anxious to hear, manage them. But manipulation sounds so crass.

JONES: That's why I insist on using the term. Only when it's out in the open can you see what it takes to survive in an organization.

SAM: So your true style is manipulation, is it? Is that the established center of your existence?

JONES: Maybe it is. I guess I believe in it because I see it wherever I look.

SAM: Well, at least I see your point now. You want to survive in the present system so you find out what makes the present system float. When you've done that, you arrange things so that you float along with it. If you want to call such realistic arrangements manipulation, I'm willing to admit the term into my vocabulary. We're all manipulators. We have to be if we want to stay alive in a manipulative system.

JONES: Why should I have the last word, Sam? You've just had it.

INDEX

256 *Index*